Be a Top Global Leader!
You Don't Need To Be A Genius!

Forty Two
Management Tips

For Top Global Leaders

Samuel L. Dunn

EMETH PRESS
www.emethpress.com

Forty Two Management Tips
for Global Top Leaders

(ISBN 9781609471002)

Library of Congress Control Number: 2016944565

Contents

Introduction

Dunn is a businessman who has worked in education for most of his career. His career in leadership and management in universities spans a quarter of a century. Also, during those years he taught graduate level management courses that integrated various business disciplines.

Over the years Dunn wrote many essays expressing his views on various business topics. Many of those essays were given to students who provided their critiques on the topic at hand. The students were typically ones with significant management experience who could add their real-life perspective to the topic. These essays have been edited to form the heart of this book. The essays reflect Dunn's philosophy of leadership, management, work, and ethics.

Dunn holds the PhD degree in mathematics and the DBA degree in International Business.

This volume is dedicated to Dunn's wife, Lois Dunn. She has been supportive of Dunn's work throughout his career. Her support in developing this series of books has been invaluable, including her editing of the essays and her comments about the content. She is a supporter of global activities, having been born in Guatemala and living there until she came to the States for college. Without her support over the years, Dunn's career would not have taken the course it did nor could it have been so successful.

Best wishes as you read these essays. May they be a stimulus for thought and conversation, and may they help you be a better leader, citizen, and global entrepreneur.

Chapter 1

Let's Go Abroad

Going Global?

Do you want to globalize your business? There may be markets in another country that would enjoy having access to your products and services, so look into adding foreign activities to your domestic operations.

Before you begin work in another country there are several questions you should explore, and information you should gather. Here are a few of the questions.

1. Will you be operating in another language?
2. Is your business legal in the target country?
3. What hoops do you need to jump through to make your firm legal in that country?
4. Are you going in with a local partner, or as a greenfield or brownfield enterprise?
5. Have you tested the market for your product?
6. How will you handle local politics and local understandings about facilitation payments?
7. Is there a labor force available?
8. What banking system can you use?
9. Can you repatriate profits?
10. Can you find suppliers?
11. How will you market your product in the country?
12. Must you run a union shop in the target country?
13. Are you sending expatriates to run the business, or will you use local leadership?

Before you begin, you may want to do a Country Risk Analysis. There are several companies in the United States that provide Country Risk Analysis services. Another source of information is the U.S. Department of Commerce. If you are borrowing money from a bank to start your international business, the bank may want to do a country risk analysis as well.

Going global will present a myriad of challenges, but potential profits may be worth the risks.

Going Global: Where to Start

If you want to globalize, where do you start? What country do you want to go to first?

One of the major reasons for failure of international expansion is failure to succeed in the new culture. Working in a different culture is more problematic than it looks at first blush. That being the case, it would be good to expand into a country that has a culture similar to yours.

This essay is written with the United States as the home culture. The author suggests the first choice of a country to expand to is Canada. Not just anywhere in Canada, but western Canada.

Why western Canada? First, the language is English. Working in your home language reduces all sorts of communication problems with government officials, suppliers, buyers, and employees. Second, western Canada has a system of laws that is transparent and based on common law, the same as the United States. While many of the laws are somewhat different, you will be able to understand the laws, and why the laws are put in place. Third, societal values are quite similar to U.S. values. The world view of most western Canadians is quite similar to the world view held by most United States citizens.

Fourth, it is close. You can get to most major cities in western Canada in just a few hours. When at your Canadian site you will still be relatively close to your home business site and to your families and friends in the United States. Fifth, you *will* have to cross a national boundary. That means you will have to deal with import-export laws and all the laws, regulations, and paperwork attendant to moving goods and services across country borders. This will give you much needed experience with this facet of international business.

Sixth, you will get experience working with a different currency. You will need to learn accounting rules which are somewhat different. You will learn how to translate financial statements from U.S. rules to Canadian rules, and back.

Once you have been successful in working in western Canada, then consider moving on to French speaking Canada. This will add another complexity to your business, but it will give you experience moving to a different language area and working with people with a somewhat different world perspective.

After conquering both sides of Canada, then consider moving to another country that is one more step removed from United States business practice. You might consider moving to a western European country. Once successful there, then on to the rest of the world.

What's the Advantage?

Why do countries trade?

Lots of theories have been given to explain why countries trade, but the two theories of *absolute advantage* and *comparative advantage* go a long way in explaining international trade. Let's take a look at these two explanations.

For absolute advantage, let's consider the case of two countries, Lower Slobovia (Slobovia) and Upper New Roscot (Roscot). It turns out that Slobovia has lots of clay that can be used to make pottery and tiles. Slobovia is a desert country with hardly any forests. Now Roscot doesn't have much clay that is good for making pottery and tiles, but it does have lots of forests and timber. Roscot is really good at making wooden furniture and lumber for houses. Here we have a situation where Slobovia needs furniture and housing, and Roscot needs pottery and tiling. Slobovia has an absolute advantage over Roscot in pottery and tiling, while Roscot has an absolute advantage over Slobovia in wooden furniture and lumber. Slobovia doesn't have timber and Roscot has poor clay to make pottery and tile. So these two countries begin to trade with each other, trading pottery and tiles for furniture and lumber.

For comparative advantage, the situation is a bit more complex. Let's suppose now Slobovia makes cars and goat milk. Also, Roscot makes cars and goat milk. They each have US$1 million that can be spent in production of cars and goat milk. Each country can use enough cars and goat milk to spend its entire US$1 million for goat milk or cars.

Suppose further that it takes Slobovia US$50,000 to produce a car and US$5 to produce one gallon of goat milk. Roscot, on the other hand, can produce a car for US$40,000 but it cost it US$8 to produce one gallon of goat milk. Thus Roscot has a comparative advantage in producing cars while Slobovia has a comparative advantage in producing goat milk.

Given this situation, Slobovia should produce only goat milk, and can produce 200,000 gallons. If it tries to produce cars, every car it produces reduces the amount of goat milk by 10,000 gallons. Roscot, on the other hand, should produce only cars, and can produce 25 cars for the US$1 million.

Given that Slobovia should produce only goat milk and Roscot should produce only cars, the two countries can then start trading with each other. Slobovia can sell goat milk to Roscot and Roscot can sell cars to Slobovia.

Country Risk Analysis

Once you have tentatively picked a country where you want to take your business, it would be a good idea to do a country risk analysis of that target country. You will need to know the risks you will face and what you might do to mitigate those risks.

Here's a short list of risk categories you will want to investigate, no matter what country you enter:

Government Stability

Administrative stability Policy stability

Military interventions Guerilla action

Breakaway regions

Financial and Economic Policies

GDP Per capital GDP

Foreign debt Exchange rate stability

Inflation Corruption

Confiscatory taxes Protection payments

Import-export duties Unbalanced budgets

Repatriation of profits Underground economy

Religious Conflict

Environmental Risks

Water Air

Earthquakes Volcanos

Floods Disease

Labor Relations

Unavailable skills Union status

Union representation in management

Legal Environment

Corporate structures Registration of corporations available

Legal requirements for business category Nationalization, confiscation

Cancellation and forced renegotiation of contracts

Doing Business

Time to establish business Costs to establish business

Obtaining land and buildings Obtaining services

Country Infrastructure

Roads Railroads

Highways Airports

Socioeconomic Conditions

Law and Order

Cultural Considerations

High Context Low Context

Power Arrangements Individualism

Masculine-feminine Long term orientation

Ethnic Tensions

Selective discrimination

Quality of Bureaucracy

You can conduct the study yourself, but it may be better to employ the services of a company which conducts risk analysis studies on a regular basis. A report on a single country is relatively inexpensive, so it may be better and less expensive to use an outside group for the study. Some of the groups which conduct such studies are:

PRS Group

Business Environmental Risk Intelligence

Economist Intelligence Unit

Euromoney

Moody's Investors Services

S.J. Rundt & Associates

Standard & Poor's Ratings Group

Also, if you are planning to borrow money from a lending institution to start business in another country, the lender may conduct its own risk analysis and you may be able to get access to the findings.

Once you have identified the risks, you will want to analyze each risk and determine if anything should be or can be done to mitigate the risk. One possibility, of course, is to purchase insurance. A few companies which provide various types of insurance are:

Lloyd's of London

The Overseas Private Investment Corporation

AON

International Risk Management Institute

World Bank Group

Whatever you do, do not go into a country blind. Take plenty of time to study all aspects of the country's political, economic, sociological, legal, technical, and natural environments before making a commitment to enter. If you decide to enter and an exhaustive study has been done and the risks mitigated, you can be more assured that success is possible.

Modes of Entry

A businessperson who wants to go global has many modes of entry into the global marketplace. The entry can begin small without too much up-front cost. Or the entry can be done with a partner in a target country. Or the entry can be done by going abroad, starting a business there from scratch in the target country. In this essay several modes of globalizing are considered.

Passive Exporting

Your business in your home country may have a web site that is located by someone in another country. That person contacts you and seeks to purchase some of your goods or services. You allow the sale to go through and you are now a globalizing business. You didn't seek out the foreign business; it came your way.

Active Exporting

In this mode of entry you want to export your goods and services. You begin to advertise in one or more foreign countries, or get an agent to market for you in the foreign countries. When orders come in, you send your products abroad and complete sales at a distance.

Sales Contract

One version of a sales contract is that you locate a buyer for your goods in another country which will buy your goods and then re-sell them in the buyer's region. The buyer might be a big box store in the other country.

Consignment Contract

With a consignment contract you locate an agent in another country who will receive your products and agree to sell them for you. You get paid for the products as the agent sells those products.

Licenses

You may give a license to a buyer in the foreign country to be your agent in that country. The license will specify the privileges and responsibilities that agent has with respect to your product.

Franchise

You may franchise your product in another country by establishing franchises that will be in a contractual relationship with you. Your contract will normally put many controls on the product delivery by that agent, including signage, quality control, pricing, and employment practices.

Equity Alliance

In an equity alliance you buy part of a company in the target country.

Brownfield Acquisition

In a Brownfield acquisition you acquire an existing business in the foreign country, take it over, and run it yourself.

Greenfield Entry

In a Greenfield entry you move into the foreign company and start a business from scratch. You build whatever facilities or plants are needed, establish a workforce, buy supplies, and start to produce and sell your product.

Finally, there is a *Joint Venture.* This is one of the most common ways of entering another country. In the joint venture your corporation and a local corporation in that foreign country form a new corporation, the joint venture. One of the advantages of the joint venture is that it normally employs leaders from that target country who know the language, the culture, the laws, and have their networks which can be used to benefit the joint venture corporation.

It should also be pointed out that many joint ventures fail for a variety of reasons. One of the entering firms may have achieved its goals and doesn't need the joint venture. There may be strong disagreements between the two forming corporations, or one side may steal intellectual property from the other. Some researchers claim that over 50% of joint ventures fail.

Getting Foreign Customers Using the U.S. Department of Commerce

Once you have decided to go international with your business, you need to decide how to enter foreign markets. One approach is to move part of your operations to a foreign country. Or maybe you will set up a sales office in the target country. In any case, you need to find buyers of your products.

You can find buyers on your own. You can advertise, use a sales team and the social media, or work your contact network. Another significant resource that's available is the U.S. Department of Commerce which provides many services to U.S. businesses whichwant to do business outside the United States.

One of the services the Department provides is Trade Event Services. This would include such events as counseling services, support at international trade shows, seminars and webinars, and trade conferences.

The Department also sponsors Export Finance Seminars. These are set up to teach exporters, lawyers, and financiers how to meet financing needs of businesses conducting foreign business. Included are seminars for Trade Financing Solutions, Exporter Symposia, and

Women and Minority Business Opportunities. The Department can help sellers identify banks which make equity investments in business ventures.

If one is shipping goods abroad, one has to manage the logistics and legalities of exporting. The Department can help one identify Export Management Companies which can assist companies in meeting the challenges of transporting goods and services abroad.

Trade missions are common ways for businesses to meet foreign businesspersons. Many times these are organized by states, and the governor of the state will take to a target country key business leaders and representatives of companies desiring to begin foreign work. On such a trip the businessperson will have opportunity to talk with leading businesspersons in the foreign country visited. Also, it can often be arranged that the U.S. businessperson can meet with potential buyers in the country.

Last, a very important program the Department has is the Gold Key program. In this program the Department arranges for U.S. businesspersons to meet with potential business partners in the foreign country. A Department representative in the targeted foreign country will identify potential business partners, then help set up meetings between the U.S. businessperson and those potential partners. The cost for the Gold Key service depends on the size of the U.S. company. For large companies, for one day, the cost at the time of this writing is $2,300, and the second day cost is $1,000. For small and medium companies the costs for first and second day Gold Key Service are $700 and $300, respectively. Of course, the U.S. businessperson has to travel to the foreign country for the meeting, and so travel expenses must be considered.

The Gold Key service can be quite impressive in the foreign country. The potential partner in the targeted country learns that the U.S. Department of Commerce is arranging the meeting, and the U.S. government involvement is remarkable to potential buyers.

The U.S. Export-Import Bank

Once you decide you want to do active exporting of your goods or services, you may need funds to get your operations off the ground. Businesses may raise funding through stock sales, sales of bonds, and borrowing. Your local bank may be able to provide some funding. However, it may be that you cannot raise from any private source the amounts needed, so you may need to look to the U.S. Federal government for assistance. If so, one organization to look to is the Export-Import Bank of the United States (EXIM).

EXIM was started by President Franklin Roosevelt in 1934. While named the Export-Import Bank, it doesn't support import assistance. Its purpose is to provide loans, loan guarantees, and insurance to foreign companies so they can buy U.S. goods. Many times those companies cannot get funding from the private sector, so EXIM steps in with assistance. EXIM backed $27+ billion in exports in fiscal 2014, and profited more that $650 million with its work; the profits go to the U.S. Treasury. EXIM reports that its default rate is less than 1%. In FY2014 assistance was given to 3,347 small businesses in the average amount of $1.5 million. EXIM was reauthorized in 2015 for the four years ending with the close of FY2019.

The United States has been in a negative balance of trade position for many years. The more the United States exports, the better the balance of trade will be. Also, exporting U.S. products provides sales and jobs for U.S. organizations. EXIM gives support to organizations that will be buying U.S. products, allowing the United States to better compete against nations that provide support to their industries.

The EXIM Internet site (http://www.exim.gov) lists some of the services provided. EXIM supports trade transactions of U.S.-made goods and services. EXIM provides: export credit insurance for exporters; pre-export working capital; direct loans to qualified small businesses; loan guarantees to lenders; foreign buyer loan guarantees to lenders for medium-term financing; co-financing with other export credit agencies; supply chain financing support; and structured trade and project finance transactions.

EXIM doesn't: support military or defense-related sales; provide grants; support the import of goods and services; support start-ups sales; support crude oil sales; give personal loans; provide financing for the purchase of land; nor finance exports to restricted countries.

To get started with EXIM, go to: http://www.exim.gov/get-started

Paying and Getting Paid

Once you have found customers and set up a contract to sell your goods, you need to determine how you are going to get paid. If you get paid immediately, well and good. But often the payment or payments will come months, or even years, later.

When payments from a foreign buyer are postponed into the future you are faced with currency concerns. What currency will be used for the payment? What will be the value of your home currency when the payment is due? What will be the value of the foreign buyer's currency when the payment is due? These matters should be taken into consideration when the payment contract is written, so that both the seller and buyer can be protected. Companies which don't plan well can lose substantial sums of money because of failure to take exchange rates, current and future, into account.

Timing of payments is an important activity of a company's treasury. Of course, these decisions also impact other areas of work, such as marketing. Customers will have preferred ways and times to pay.

It is helpful to consider some examples of future payments and how changes in exchange rates can impact payments. Suppose Outback Steel in the United States sells $10,000,000 worth of steel to Edelweis Fabricators in Switzerland on January 8. On January 8 the exchange rate is $1=SF1.3885. Thus the value of the sale is SF13,885,000. Terms of the sale call for payment in six months of SF13,885,000. These terms were established at the request of the buyer, which wanted to pay in its own currency. Now suppose we are six months later on July 8. Suppose now the exchange rate is $1=SF1.3833. Then Outback Steel will receive $10,037,591. Thus Outback Steel gained $37,591 on its $10,000,000 sales, through these six months. On the surface it looks good for Outback, but we don't know what is happening to the dollar currency in the United States during those six months; what was the inflation rate? Thus Outback may or may not be better off.

As a second example, the exchange rates may swing the other direction. Suppose Outback Steel sells $10,000,000 worth of steel to Edelweis Fabricators of Switzerland on January 8 when $1=SF1.3885, with payment to be made in six months in Swiss Francs. So Edelweis will owe SF13,885,000. Now suppose six months later on July 8 the exchange rate is $1=SF1.3901. Then Outback Steel will receive $9,988,490.37. Thus Outback Steel lost $11,509.63.

As a third example, suppose Outback Steel sells $10,000,000 worth of steel to Edelweis Fabricators of Switzerland on January 8, when the exchange rate is $1=SF1.3885. Payment is to be made in six months in Swiss Francs, so the payment will be SF13,885,000. Suppose on January 8 the six-months forward rate is $1=SF1.3901. Suppose further that the exchange rate on July 8 is exactly what the forward rate was predicted on January 8. In other words, the Swiss Franc has depreciated against the U.S. dollar. As given in the second example, Outback Steel will receive $9,988,490.37, for a nominal loss of $11,509.63.

Now Outback Steel, when making the sale, does not know for sure what the exchange rate will be on July 8. It does have the six-months forward rate to work with, which predicts the Swiss Franc will depreciate against the U.S. dollar. Outback Steel can mitigate against exchange rate risk by wisely using various kinds of financial instruments.

To continue this thought, Outback Steel can get some protection by buying on January 8 an option to sell Swiss Francs on July 8 at the predicted exchange rate of $1=SF1.3901. When Edelweis pays on July 8, Outback Steel can exercise its option if it desires and guarantee that its loss will be no more than $11,509.63.

So suppose Outback Steel did indeed buy the option. Then the actual loss will depend on the spot rates on July 8. Suppose the spot rate on July 8 is $1=SF1.3910. Then the SF13,885,000 will result in a dollar payment of $9,982,027.32, for a loss of 17,972.68. In that case Outback Steel will exercise its option and restrict its loss to only $11,509.63.

If Outback Steel buys the option, it is said to be *hedging* for the future. Hedging is a financial transaction designed to counterbalance another transaction so as to protect against risk. A management decision must be made as to whether to hedge or not, for hedging, such as buying the option described above, will cost money. Some firms, if working between two fairly stable currencies, will not hedge if the payment date is soon, but will hedge if the payment or payments are many months or years later.

Translating Financial Statements

Don't confuse financial statement translation with currency exchange transactions. In currency exchange transactions one is changing one currency for another. In financial statement translation one is taking the financial statements given in one currency and moving those statements into another currency.

For purposes of this essay, suppose your company is based in the United States and you have a subsidiary business in Mexico. In Mexico at the end of each accounting period you develop a profit and loss statement and a balance sheet for your Mexican operations. You then need to send this information to the parent company in the United States for the parent company to consolidate the Mexican report into its overall financial statements for that period.

Making the translation from statements denominated in Mexican currency, the Peso, to United States dollars calls for decisions on the part of the company's treasury. The first major decision is to determine the functional currency of the subsidiary. Is the functional currency the U.S. dollar or the currency of the subsidiary country? In our example, is the functional currency in which the subsidiary carries on its day-to-day business the Mexican Peso or the US Dollar? The functional currency would be the local currency if a majority of the cash it works with is received and spent in the local currency. The subsidiary must keep records in its functional currency.

There are two methods to use in translating financial statements, the *current method* and the *temporal method*. If the functional currency is the same as the home currency, the current method is use. Otherwise the temporal method is used. The following description about the two methods is adapted from the Eisneramper web site: www.eisneramper.com /Foreign-Currency-Translation-FAS-53.aspx.

Current Method

The Current Method translates liabilities and assets at the current spot rate on the translation day. "Retained earnings are translated at the weighted-average rate for the relevant year, with the exception of any components that are identifiable with specific dates, in which case the spot rates for those dates are used." "Equity items, other than retained earnings, are translated at the spot rates in effect on each related transaction date." "Income statement items are translated at the average rate for the period, except where specific identification is practicable."

Temporal Method

In the temporal method, "nonmonetary balance sheet accounts and related income statement accounts are re-measured using historical exchange rates. The resulting translation adjustment is recognized in current earnings."

Managing Expatriate Workers

Is there a foreign assignment in your future? Or will you be managing employees who are assigned to an overseas billing? Either way, you need to know some of the principal concerns involved in foreign assignments.

There are many problems with expatriate assignments. The failure rate is high; various studies show failure rates from 10% to 40%.

Further, failure is costly, with typical costs being over $100,000 per failure. Failure leads to disruption of jobs, families, and careers, so it behooves a company sending a worker abroad to prepare the company and worker well for the assignment.

There is some terminology that should be recognized. *Expatriates* are the workers sent to work in another country. *Host Country Nationals* are the people in the receiving country. *Home Country Nationals* are the people in the sending country. *Parent Country Nationals* are the workers in the country of the parent company. *Inpatriates* are people send from another country back to the home country. Finally, *Globalites* are workers who spend most of their careers as expatriates working in one or more foreign countries.[1]

Expatriate workers may be classified by the amount of time spent abroad. There are short-term, long-term, frequent flyer, and commuter expatriates.

Expatriate workers may be assigned abroad for many reasons. Among them are: to start up operations; to provide technical assistance; to give international experience; to provide coordination; because talent is unavailable in the foreign country; because the company views the foreign duties as short lived; and the company may want to maintain a foreign image in the host country.

The pattern of expatriates varies by country, and is sometimes controlled by law. For example, Brazil expects that two thirds of employees in foreign-owned companies will be Brazilian citizens. While U.S. firms indeed send out expatriates, there is a tendency to use local citizens in the host country where possible, because they are familiar with the culture, know the language, are less expensive, and it's good public relations.

Corporations have different orientations about international assignments. Some corporations are *ethnocentric*, in which the orientation is to the home company and country. Only home nationals are used for senior assignments. Foreign assignments are not typically viewed as good for a person's career. Typically there is not much training, and the host country language is not required. Assessment of the expatriates is based on home country standards.

At the other end of the spectrum are the *globalcentric* companies. These companies assign their best people for international work, and the international work is viewed as important for job advancement.

---

[1]Resources: Hodgetts, R.M. & Luthans, F. (2000). *International Management.* Irwin McGraw-Hill

Much time is spent in selection, training, and assessment of expatriate workers. Compensation is good, and long-term assignments are common. Assessment is based on the particular assignment.

In developing policies for expatriate assignment, the following characteristics are recommended for the policies. They should be gender neutral and graduated by length of out-of-country assignment. They should make the expatriate whole in terms of compensation and career advancement. The policies should provide for all aspects of living in the foreign country, and should prepare for re-entry to the home country and firm.

In selecting individuals for expatriate assignments, several criteria should be considered. The individuals should have: flexibility; ability to adapt; tolerance for ambiguity; technical competence; human relations skills; a desire to serve abroad; academic qualifications; and have a desire to learn the target country's culture. A plus would be if the individual knows the language of the target country [from Hodgetts & Luthans, and Tu].[2] Expatriates should have independence and self-reliance and good health.

Indicators of adaptability would be: work experience in other cultures; previous overseas travel; knowledge of a foreign language; sensitivity to fine differences in culture; and flexibility in managing operations.

An especially important requirement for expatriate assignment is family adaptability. One of the significant reasons for assignment failure is failure of the spouse to adapt to the foreign culture.

If the assignment is long term and the spouse and family go with the worker, the spouse may have to give up his or her job. Further, the spouse may not have permission to work in the host country, and thus can get bored after a few months.

Children will need to be placed in school in the foreign country. Many times this will be a private international school which teaches partly in the home country's language. Tuition may be quite high. Also, there is the matter of getting the children to and from the school, which may be problematic in some countries where criminal activity is high.

Many expatriates will suffer culture shock in the new culture. They may be working in a culture with a very different world view, where ways of doing things are different, the food is different, the relation-

---

[2]Tu, H. (1994). Preparing yourself for an international assignment. *Business Horizons 37(1)*, 67-70.

ships between managers and employees may be different, and the language may be different. These differences may cause much frustration to the expatriate worker. Some expatriates may never adjust and will need to return home. Or it may be that the worker adjusts but the spouse and/or children do not.

Preparing the expatriate worker for the move abroad is very important. It would be good for the worker and spouse to visit the foreign country before the assignment is finalized. They can talk to other expatriates to learn what life is like in that country. On the trip they can check into housing, schooling, health care, and general living conditions. If the visit goes well and the assignment is made, the worker can read books, watch videos, start reading the newspapers of the foreign country, and generally acquaint himself or herself with the assignment.

Expatriate assignments cost money. The total cost may be two or three times the compensation of the worker at home. Here are some of the costs:

Training

Moving the family

Relocation allowance

Cost of housing

Compensation for lifestyle differences

Incentives of international assignment

Hardship allowance in some countries

Home-leave travel allowances for family

Tax equalization

Education for children

In-country transportation

Insurance: travel, disability, health, life

Repatriation costs

Tax equalization may or may not be costly. The United States has tax treaties with many, but not all, countries so that worker income is not double taxed. The company's lawyers should investigate this matter thoroughly and make appropriate adjustments to compensation so the worker is made whole.

It has been reported that approximately 20% of expatriates leave their jobs in the first year after returning. Preparation should be made in advance for repatriation of the worker when his or her foreign assignment is completed. This can be a difficult time for the employee. He or she has been away from the home assignment. The home job may have been given to another employee in the absence. The employee is not up on the gossip. There may be a new boss. There may not be a clear-cut job assignment waiting. There may even be trouble locating an office for the returning employee.

The returning employee may experience reverse culture shock involving the family, company, and general culture. In the foreign assignment the expatriate may have had more authority and autonomy on the job. Back at home the returning expatriate may be just another of many people at the same authority and autonomy level; this may take much adjustment.

Then the returning employee has to get used to new living arrangements. In the foreign country the expatriate worker may have lived in a gated community, may have had maid service, and a driver to take the expatriate to work, to drive the children to school, and drive the spouse as needed. Most of these perks will not be available at home, so the whole family social contract will need to be re-negotiated.

There are many challenges related to expatriate assignments. However, the assignment may be a wonderful experience for the worker and the worker's family. It may be so good that the worker will want to stay for many years or be assigned to another foreign country. If the company prepares well and takes good care of the expatriate worker and family, the chances of success will be significantly higher.

Globalization

Globalization is the process of increasing cross-border relationships involving economics, business, technology transfer, political engagement, immigration, personal contact, medicine, education, and other aspects of culture.

Globalization is here to stay. As travel becomes easier, as technologies allow us to communicate immediately around the globe, as corporations move operations into other countries, the world is continuously globalizing.

Most countries around the world are getting into the globalization act; it is no longer the domain of the developed countries. In 1955 75 of the 100 largest businesses in the world were from the United States;

now the number is less than 25. More than US$3 trillion moves every day in foreign exchange markets. Stock exchanges, large or small, are now found in almost all countries. The U.S. Dollar, the Euro, and the Japanese Yen are now considered to be strong reserve currencies.

Various companies have developed indices to assess countries' levels of globalization. One such company is A.T. Kearney which has its Globalization Index. In this Index the Kearney firm considers four sectors. The Technology sector involves the number of Internet users, Internet hosts, and secure servers. The Political Engagement sector counts the number of memberships in international organizations, participation in United Nations Security Council missions, and the number of foreign embassies hosted. The Personal Contacts sector counts international travel and tourism, international telephone traffic, and cross-border transfers. The Economic Integration sector considers trade, foreign direct investment, capital flows, and income payments and receipts.

In its 2014 analysis, the KOF firm, which studies globalization, found the countries most globalized in order were: Ireland, Belgium, Netherlands, Austria, Singapore, Denmark and Sweden. The United States was #32 on the list. The Russian Federation was #56, and the People's Republic of China was #72.

Surface Culture

Some argue that cultures around the world are converging. After all, men in Russia, France and the United States wear shirts and ties. People in all three countries eat French Fries. People in all three countries watch television and have cell phones. So obviously, cultures are merging.

But not so fast. This argument comes from looking at surface phenomena. Maybe surface cultures are merging, but that doesn't get at deep culture. Deep culture involves world view, religion, attitudes about the family, work, and the government. There is far less evidence that deep cultures are converging.

Whether converging or not, businesspersons wanting to do international business must know the surface culture of the countries in which they are working. Fortunately, surface culture can be learned fairly easily; not so for deep culture. Learning the surface culture can be done by reading about the culture, watching videos, reading that country's newspapers, talking with people from the culture, and by direct observation. Numerous books have been written about almost any country around the world, so you can read how life and business are conducted in the country of interest.

Scholars have developed several ways of looking at surface cultures, and have classified cultures using various criteria. When discussing the characteristics of a culture below, it should be pointed out that these are general observations; a given individual in the culture may be quite different from the general culture.

Let's take a look at several of these modes of classification. The first category is *Paralanguage*. This refers to the way people talk in a country. What are the rate, pitch, volume, and use of pauses? Is speaking loud, soft, fast, or slow? Arabs generally speak strong and sincerly. Italians speak rapidly. People from the South in the United States generally speak more slowly than their northern counterparts.[3]

Another category is *Metacommuication*, which refers to the importance of social context for the words. Consider this sentence: You look nice today. Is that a compliment or an insult? It depends on the context. The number of people you bring to a negotiation may send a signal of the importance of the discussions to your counterparts.

Chronemics is the attitude toward use of time. The attitude may be *monochronic*; if so, the holder of this attitude wants to typically do one thing at a time. Or the attitude may be *polychronic*, doing many things at once. South Koreans would typically be polychronic.

Oculesics is the study of eye contact in communications. Some cultures practice direct eye contact, while others practice minimal eye contact. Some Latin Americans and the French would normally use direct eye contact, while Native Americans in the United States would use minimal eye contact.

Olfactics is the use of smell in a culture. In some countries such as the United Sates body odor is very negative; in Arab countries it may be desirable to smell a friend's body odor.

Haptics considers communication through touch. In the United States touch is reserved. In many Latin American countries touching is considered more acceptable. Male to male and female to female touching may be very acceptable in some cultures, not in others.

Chromatics is the use of color. Acceptable colors in gifts, gift-wrapping, clothing, and banners vary from country to country. Black

---

[3]Resources: Chaney, L.H., & Marin, J.S. (2000). *Intercultural Business Communication* (2nd ed.). Prentice-Hall. www.communicaid.com/cross-cultural training/blog/chronemics/www.immersion.com/haptics-technology/what-is-haptics/http://www.fb9dv.uni-duisburg.de/ti/en/education/teaching/ss07/multiculti/presentation%203.pdf

is often used to signify mourning or death in the United States, while white would signify mourning and death in Japan. Brides often wear white in the United States, but red or yellow in India. Green should not be used for gifts in Egypt, for that is the color of the national flag.

Proxemics is communication through use of space. Different cultures have unspoken understandings about how close one should stand to another person while engaged in conversation. As a general observation, people in developed countries stand further apart than persons in underdeveloped countries.

Kinesics is communication through posture and gesture. In some cultures it is not considered good to show too much emotion to strangers. Gestures vary widely. People in the United States are moderate in their use of gestures, while Arabs typically have wide gestures with arms and elbows out.

Gestures can quickly get one in trouble. Many common gestures used in the United States are considered obscene on various places around the world. Gestures such as Thumbs Up, the OK Sign, and the Texas Longhorns gesture would be considered bad in many places. The Middle Finger salute is almost universally considered to be obscene.

In addition to these categories, four other matters should be mentioned. First is the use of business cards. When doing business abroad it is good to use both sides of the card. On one side print the information in the language of your home country, and on the other side print the information using the language of the target country.

Be careful how you present your business card to another businessperson. Typically give it with both hands and treat it reverently. When receiving a business card, receive it with both hands, read it, comment about it, and lay it respectfully on the table in front of you, or put it in a gold card carrier and place it in your coat pocket near your heart.

Second is male-female behavior. Be extremely careful with your interactions with the opposite gender. In some cultures it would not be desirable to shake hands or to be alone with a member of the opposite sex. Keep your business very professional and not personal.

Third is toilet behavior. In many places around the world you will need to pay to go the toilet. Or the toilet may be free but you will need to pay for toilet paper. In some places toilets are open to both men and women. In others there may be a unisex bathroom but persons from the opposite sex will be cleaning the bathroom. In some countries the toilet may be nothing more than a hole in the floor or ground.

Fourth, watch the use of your hands. When shaking hands, use only your right hand. When giving something to another person, use only your right hand or use both hands. Typically you would never hand something with your left hand. The rationale for this is that in many countries the left hand is used for cleaning oneself after using the toilet. The hand is considered contaminated and should not be used alone for polite communication.

Managing in a High Context Culture

About two-thirds of the world's people live in high context cultures. This involves most Africans, Latin Americans, and Asians. People from the United States, Canada, northern Europe, and Australia have low context cultures.

High context cultures have the following characteristics: high importance of personal relationships; hierarchical; person oriented rather than task oriented; long term perspective; status by family or position in society. Low context cultures are characterized by: low importance of personal relationships; egalitarian; task oriented rather than person-oriented. Short term perspective; status by personal accomplishment.

Cultural values of high context societies are described by such terms as: group harmony; collectiveness; cooperation; quality; patience; belonging; respect for age/seniority; patience; indirectness; family harmony; authority; and hospitality.

As a caution, note that a particular individual in a high context society may not exhibit all the values and world view held by the general society. The characteristics given above represent the high majority of the people.

A person who comes from a low context society will face challenges managing in a high context society. Many practices, worker-management relationships, and values will be different from those in the low context society. The first difference considered is the ways employees are motivated. Maslow's hierarchy of need satisfaction appears to work fairly well in low context societies, but not in high context societies. In Maslow's hierarchy, the highest need that must be fulfilled is self-actualization. In high context societies the highest need will involve the well-being of the group, the actualization of the group. Thus rewards and recognitions that would serve well in a low-context society may not work so well in a high context society.

A second difference that may be noticed is the relationships bet-ween management and the worker. In low context societies workers tend to want to work fairly independently of their managers. The pre-ferred interaction method is that the boss gives the employee a job to do with some instructions, then the employee does the job without too much interaction with the boss. In the high context society, the employee typically wants more interaction with the manager. The em-ployee checks in often with the manager and has open communication while the project is being completed. The manager reinforces often his/her appreciation of the employee.

A third difference relates to nepotism. In low context societies the practice of nepotism is to be avoided. A manager should not manage his/her own relatives. It is viewed that the manager cannot be objec-tive in dealing with his/her relatives. In high context societies, it is generally viewed as a good to work with people from one's family, clan, tribe, or social organization. The manager knows his/her rela-tives and close acquaintances and can use family and peer pressure to assure that they perform adequately.

The concept of face is very important in most high context societies. One must manage so no one loses face. Do not cause any-one to be embarrassed in any social context. Thus employees will not publicly question the boss about the boss' words or actions. Similar-ly, if discipline must be applied to an employee, it is done privately. When going into negotiations with another person or group, find out all you can in advance about the business situation so you will not be embarrassed by failure to respond adequately. Similarly, make sure your counterpart in the negotiations has as much information as pos-sible so he/she will not be caught flatfooted and lose face. Do not raise gottcha questions that would cause loss of face.

Loyalty to one's family, clan, tribe, social group, and nation are highly prized. An insult to the family or tribe is taken personally. Ma-terial possessions are to be shared quite readily with family members. Helping family members get ahead by contributing to school tuitions or helping a business get started is quite common. You take care of them and they will take care of you.

Being rather than doing will be most important. Status comes from the family or social position rather than from personal effort. A raise in pay on the job may not cause higher performance; maybe just the opposite. With higher wages the employee may not have to work so hard or so long to maintain his/her level of living, so take the higher wage, reduce work, and enjoy life.

Why the United States Is Different from Most of the Rest of the World

About two-thirds of the people of the world live in high context cultures. Most Asians, Africans, and South Americans live in high context societies. The United States is part of the one-third that live in low context cultures. Since U.S. businesspersons are doing business all around the world, it is important that the U.S. businessperson understand how the high context cultures differ from the United States.

First consider *Maslow's Hierarchy*. Abraham Maslow developed a hierarchy of needs which describe need satisfaction. The five steps in the hierarchy are: biological and physiological needs, safety needs, love and belongingness needs, esteem needs, and self-actualization needs. This hierarchy has been used extensively as a theory behind various employee need satisfaction policies. This hierarchy was developed, and most of the research about it has been conducted, in low context societies which are generally characterized by individualism.

But most of the people of the world live in high context cultures where collectivism is the key value. For these people, group-actualization is the highest value, not self-actualization. An example of this is the *I Ching* philosophy of China, a 2000-year-old philosophy that has a hierarchy of nine levels. The highest levels ascribe the top values to the group, not the individual.

Another difference is the view of *abstract law*. In high context cultures it is typical that the highest allegiance goes to the family, the clan, the tribe, the worker's firm, the student's school. The government is way down the list. If a conflict arises between serving the family or obeying the abstract law passed by some strangers down in the capital, allegiance may be given to the family.

The next matter to be considered is *nepotism*. In most low context cultures nepotism is considered to be a negative management practice. Not so in most high context cultures where personal relationships are considered most important. In those cultures you would hire your family members or relatives because you know them and know their strengths and weaknesses. Further, if those family members misperform on the job, you can bring to bear the pressure of the family to get them to shape up their work. Finally, you owe allegiance to your family and close networks. If a job is available and they need work, give it to them rather than some stranger you don't know.

Plagiarism is considered bad, and maybe even illegal, in most low-context cultures. Ideas belong to the person who generated the idea;

it is that person's intellectual property. Use of those ideas should be acknowledged and credit given to the creator. In some high-context cultures being quoted without attribution would be considered a compliment; it doesn't need to be cited.

Argumentum ad hominem is considered bad, especially by academics in low-context cultures. If an idea is presented, it is to be assessed on its merits, not on the person who advanced the idea. Arguing against the provider of the idea is call argumentum ad hominem (argument against the man). In some high-context cultures, the idea is to be assessed along with the presenter. If the presenter is not illustrating in his or her own life, if the presenter is not walking the walk as well as talking the talk, then the idea may be dismissed as unrealistic or undoable. If the presenter of the idea doesn't even embrace it enough to embody it is his or her own life, then the idea is not worthy of consideration.

The *Law of the Excluded Middle* is a thought tool used especially in western cultures that have been influenced by Greek philosophy. It says that Idea A and Idea Not A cannot happen simultaneously. Idea A and Idea Not A would be considered to be in conflict; it would represent a contradiction. A person who holds both simultaneously would be thought to be illogical. In some cultures, however, contradictions are not necessarily thought to be illogical; contradictions can be held simultaneously. In fact, some would argue that one cannot get a full picture of a matter unless there are contradictions involved. One well-known expression of this logical approach would be the *ying* and *yang* of Chinese philosophy.

Finally, we get to the notion of *corruption*. Just by using the term we have already poisoned the wells because the term has so many negative connotations. The point to be made here is that what is considered corruption in low-context, particularly developed countries, may not be considered evil in other countries. What some may view as corruption may just be considered payments for services and may be the normal way of doing business. The message to the U.S. businessperson is to not fall into the trap of viewing a given business transaction as evil just because it involves a payment for service. Judge each instance on its own merits.

Black and Gray Markets

All economies have an underground economy, or *black market*. A black market trade is one in which the trade is illegal. The goods or services may not be illegal to own, but the trade itself is illegal. Most times the goods or services being traded on the black market can be bought or sold on the legal market, otherwise known as a *white market*. Another type of market is the *gray market*, in which goods or services are sold in a way not intended by the creator of the goods or services.[4]

All sorts of goods and services may be sold through the black market. Prominent are illegal drugs, weapons, medicines, exotic animals and animal parts, money and money instruments. Also part of the black market would be the practice of starting a business without registering the business, all in order to avoid paying required wages, or paying taxes, or contributing to state social welfare funds. There is also a black market in sale of human parts, especially kidneys.

Much criminal activity is part of the black market. Prostitution, sexual slavery, drug operations are normally carried on in violation of the law, or without proper registration, or by hiding transactions through cash only dealings. Sometimes a bartering economy may be part of the black market. Economic activity that is not reported, and/or is carried on in cash so no reports need to be filed, would normally be considered part of the black market.

If a country fixes the exchange rate of its currency vis-à-vis another major currency such as the U.S. dollar, a black market in that currency may arise. Many times travelers to such countries will be button-holed by currency sellers on the streets who are willing to sell the local currency at rates better than the official rates. It is often tempting to buy the currency that way, but one should always be alert for counterfeit money.

The extent of the black market varies from country to country. Two economists, Ceyhun Elgin and Oguz Oztunali, studied the size of underground economies from 2005 to 2009. They estimated 22.67% of the world GDP was in the underground economy. They also observed that the percentage of the economy that was underground was typically higher in poor countries than in rich countries. In terms of country groupings, Elgin and Oztunali found that the mean percentage of the countries' GDP of the shadow economies in Latin American countries was 41.98%, in Sub-Saharan countries it was 43.06%, and in Asia it was 43.06%. In OECD-EU countries the percentage was 17.84%.

Friedrich Schneider studied shadow economies around the world. Writing in 2007 he found the shadow economies as a percentage of

[4]Resources:http://www.voxeu.org/article/shadow-economies-around-world-model-based-estimates

official GDP in 2004/2005 was 51.1% in the Republic of Congo, 52.2% in Cambodia, 33.2% in Turkey, 67.2% in Bolivia, 66.4% in Georgia, and 7.9% in the United States. He found the highest percentage in an OECD country to be 26.3% in Greece.[5]

Countertrade

A very important way of conducting international trade is through countertrading. A *countertrade* is one in which trade is done partially or totally as an exchange of goods rather than as an exchange of money. According to Daniels, Radebaugh, and Sullivan, the general consensus is that countertrade is "between 10 and 20 percent of all world trade."

Daniels et al. gave some examples of countertrade. Malaysia swapped palm oil for fertilizer and machinery with North Korea. The Philippines received rice supplies from Vietnam. Pepsi-Cola delivered syrup that is paid for by Solichnaya Vodka. Early on, Pepsi took delivery of 17 submarines, a cruiser, and frigate, and a destroyer from the Russian government in payment for Pepsi products, then sold the 20 vessels for scrap steel (Daniels et al, 2011, pp. 506-507)[6]

Countertrade is quite common, but the practice varies considerably from country to country depending on local laws. Countertrade has advantages and disadvantages. One advantage is that it does not involve transfer of money payments, and hence a country's foreign currency is preserved. Further, it may give a buyer opportunity to acquire goods that the buyer would otherwise not be able to afford. A problem with countertrade is that the money equivalent value of the goods may be hard to determine, and hence accounting for the transaction may be doubtful. A second problem with countertrade is that it involves complex negotiations and is time consuming.

There are several types of countertrade. First is *barter*. In bartering there is an exchange of goods with no change of money. It is a one-time, fully completed transaction.

A second type of countertrade is *counterpurchase*. In this mode the seller or seller's country agrees to purchase goods from the buyer's country. The counterpurchase amount will typically be some per-

---

[5]Schneider, F., (2007). Shadow economies and corruption all over the world: New estimates for 145 countries. Economics (2007-9). Retrieved from http: www.economics-ejournal/org /economics/journalarticles

[6]Resource: Daniels, J.D., Radebaugh, L.H, & Sullivan, D.P. (2011). *International business: Environments and operations* (13th ed.). Boston, MA: Prentice Hall. London Countertrade Roundtable at www.londoncountertrade.org

centage of the original transaction. With the counterpurchase, the balance of payments between the two countries is not impacted so much as in a money transaction.

Buyback occurs when the sellers of equipment are not paid immediately, but are paid later when the equipment goes into production and some of the output goes back to the original seller of the equipment.

Offset Arrangements

In this arrangement, the seller of the product authorizes the buyer to assemble parts of the product in the buyer's country, or allows other producers in the buyer's country to assemble the product, or agrees to take in parts made by the buyer or in the buyer's country. This method is often used by countries purchasing military materiel.

Three-Party Arrangements

Countertrade agreements may involve parties in more than two countries. Products may be exchanged in a three-way agreement, for example, in *switch trading*. Suppose two countries have an imbalance in trade. A third country may purchase what one of the two countries needs from the other, then trade it to the first country, then exchange it for some product that the third country needs.

Islam and Islamic Finance

Islam now claims 1.5 billion adherents around the world with up to 3 million Muslims living in the United States. Since economic and business systems around the world are increasingly integrated and businesspersons from the United States will most likely be interacting at some level with Muslims, it is important that U.S. businesspersons understand Islam and Islamic finance.[7]

Islam: The Religion

Islam developed in the sixth century of the Common Era (C.E.). Islam means "surrendering one's will to the will of Allah." *Allah* is the name for God in Arabic. The first leader of Islam was Muhammad

---

[7]Trammell, S. (2005). Islamic finance. *CFA Magazine*. March-April, 16-23.

(570-633 C.E.)[8] who is viewed as the Messenger of *Allah* and the Messenger of Islam. Muhammad was born in the Arabian Peninsula. He gained influence as a businessperson and began to spread his ideas in his region. Muslims believe that Muhammad received from *Allah* through the angel Gabriel the message now written in the *Quaran*, the primary holy book in Islam. Muhammad began to gain adherents to his theology and became the first proponent of the religion now known as Islam.

History of Islam

At the death of Muhammad in 633, the area of Islamic influence was largely limited to the areas around the Middle East. Early leaders were descendants of Muhammad. In 637 Jerusalem and Syria came under the control of the Muslims. From that time until the 1400s Islam spread across North Africa into Spain and east into Northern India. In the 12th century Islam began to spread in Sumatra, Java, and Indonesia. Indonesia is now the country with the largest Muslim population in the world.

By the year 1500 Islam had largely reached the lands that it now occupies. Part of the slowdown in expansion of Islam can be laid to the colonization of many parts of the world by the European powers. In the 20th century the defeat of the Turks in World War I and the development of the Soviet Union slowed down Muslim expansion in Central Asia. The spread of Islam was essentially stopped in India in the 20th century with the partitioning of the sub-continent into India, Pakistan, and Bangladesh. Today the Central Asian countries remain mostly Muslim, as are the lands of Indonesia, Malaysia, and the southern Philippines. There are now sizable Muslim populations in western China.

Also in the 20th century there was a sizable growth in the number of Muslims in the United States. Many people from the Middle East immigrated to the United States and brought Islam with them. Also, there has been a significant growth in the number of African American converts to Islam. Many were attracted to the Nation of Islam, a variant on orthodox Islam, which was headed by Elijah Mohammad (Nation, 2008).[9]

---

[8]Nasr, S. H. (2003). *Islam: Religion, history, and civilization.* New York: HarperCollins.

[9]Nation. (2008). NOI.org: The official site of the Nation of Islam. Retrieved from http://www.noi.org

Religious Beliefs and Practices

Islam is viewed as the completion and perfection of earlier religions, especially Judaism and Christianity. The religion is based on the Muslim holy book, the *Quaran,* as well as the life, sayings, and actions of Muhammad.

The word "*Quaran*" means "the recital." The words of the *Quaran* are considered by most Muslims to have been dictated in the Arabic language to Muhammad by the angel Gabriel, and hence the words themselves are sacred. Some Muslims believe that only the Arabic words are sacred; translations cannot be sacred.

Many heroes from the Old and New Testaments, such as Adam, Noah, Abraham, Ishmael, Isaac, Lot, Jacob, Joseph, Job, Moses, Aaron, David, Solomon, Jonah, John the Baptist, and Jesus are considered to be Prophets. Jesus is given special honor, as is Mary, the Mother of Jesus. The culmination of the prophetic line is Muhammad who has by revelation of *Allah* brought the final word of truth to humankind.

Islam is a monotheistic religion. There is one God whose name in Arabic is *Allah. Allah* is the creator of all that exists. *Allah* is eternal. *Allah* is just and abhors injustice. *Allah* is all-knowing and will reward justness and punish injustice. Humans are free to choose good and evil. There will be a Day of Resurrection and Judgment at which time *Allah* will raise people from the dead, reunite their souls with their bodies, and question them about their beliefs and actions. They will then receive *Allah*'s judgment and be assigned for eternity to Heaven (Paradise) or Hell.

The purpose of life is to be tested. If one believes in *Allah* as prescribed by Islam, practices the faith, and does good, then one will be ushered into Paradise. If one has done evil, but sincerely repents, then *Allah* may forgive that person and still usher him or her into Paradise. Repentance is a private matter.

Muslims have five obligations that represent the Five Pillars of the Islamic faith. First, the Muslim must believe in *Allah* as the sole God and that Muhammad is *Allah*'s Messenger. Second Muslims are required to pray five times every day facing toward Mecca Third, Muslims must observe the month of Ramadan by not eating food and drink during the daytime, among other observances. Fourth, Muslims must give alms to those in need. Fifth, unless prohibited by health or finances, each Muslim must make a pilgrimage to Mecca at least once during his or her lifetime. Muslims use a lunar calendar, which has fewer days each year than the solar year.

World Muslim Populations

Islam is the second largest religion in terms of adherents, after Christianity. A particularly authoritative study of Muslims in the United States was conducted by the Pew Research Center and published in May 2007. That study put the number of adult Muslims in the United States at 1.5 million, with a total Muslim population of 2.35 million (Pew, 2007, p. 3).[10] "Within specific ethnic heritages, 64% of Muslims from the Arab region say they are white, while 20% say they are some other or mixed race" (p. 18).

Many people confuse Arabs with Muslims. Generally speaking, an Arab is a person who speaks Arabic. There are 22 countries which are considered to be Arabic. Iran, Iraq, Turkey, Pakistan, and Afghanistan, for example, are not Arab countries. An Arab may be an adherent of one of a wide number of religions. Muslims may or may not speak Arabic, although they are certainly encouraged to learn enough Arabic to read the *Quaran*. A 2000 study showed that "only 23% of the Arab population in the United States is actually Muslim" (ARDA, 2008, par. 36).[11]

The Sunni and Shia Division

Islam was unified so long as Muhammad was alive, but within decades after his death the Islamic world was divided into two major camps, Sunni Islam and Shia Islam. The division occurred because of differences of opinion concerning who was to lead the Muslim world. At present only about 15 percent of the world's Muslims belong to Shia Islam. They are known as Shiites. Shiites constitute a majority in Iran and Iraq. Each of the two main groupings are divided into schools.

Following the disappearance of early leaders and the realization that they were not returning, a council of Shia scholars elected a supreme Iman. The process has continued until this era. Probably the best known of the recent Iman is the Ayatollah Khomeni, who took over the government of Iran after the fall of the Shah in 1979. Amin wrote that the position of the "Shia Imam has come to be imbued with Pope-like infallibility and the Shia religious hierarchy is not dissimilar in structure and religious power to that of the Catholic Church within

---

[10]Pew. (2007, May 22). Muslim Americans. Pew Research Center.
[11]ARDA. (2000). Religious congregations and membership study, 2000. Retrieved from: http://www.thearda.com/Archive/Files /Descriptions/RCMSST.asp

Christianity" (Amin, n.d., Sec. I, par. 9).[12] The leading Ayatollah at the time of this writing is Grand Ayatollah Ali Sistani of Iraq.

The great majority, over 80%, of the world's Muslims belong to Sunni Islam. This branch of Islam rejected the notion that leadership of Islam should come from descendants of Muhammad. "Sunni Islam, in contrast [to Shia Islam], more closely resembles the myriad independent churches of American Protestantism. Sunnis do not have a formal clergy, just scholars and jurists, who may offer non-binding opinions" (Amin, n.d., par. 9).

Most Sunni and Shiite Muslims around the world recognize the other principal group as legitimate followers of Islam. There have been attempts to reconcile differences and to bring more harmony in the world-wide Islamic tradition. However, this has not halted serious dissension and even warfare among Shia and Sunni groups, often not just because of the religious differences but also from ethnic, linguistic, and economic competition.

Additional Sources of Doctrines/Practices

In addition to the *Quaran*, Muslims regard as binding the *Sunnah*, which is the collection of information as to what Muhammad "said, did, or permitted to do" (as-Siba'i, n.d., par. 6).[13]

The scholar Warde qualified the recognized sources of Muhammad's teachings by introducing the word *hadith* in connection with the Sunnah. Warde wrote that "the first [hadith] actually refers to the words and deeds of the Prophet while the second [Sunnan] refers to the tradition or path established by those words and deeds." "[T]he Sunna consists of the practices and rulings deducted from such narratives]" (Warde, 2000, p. 32).

Finally, there are the contributions of Islamic scholars over the centuries. Opinions promulgated by scholars are called *fatwas*. These four, the *Quaran*, Sunnah, hadiths, and fatwas constitute the body of rules called the *Shariah*. The Shariah is highly respected and is binding on all practicing Muslims.

Scholars from a particular tradition who have developed the fatwas from the *Quaran,* Sunnah, and Hadiths may have developed laws and rules that differ with those developed in another Islamic tradition.

---

[12]Amin, H. (n.d.). The Origins of the Sunni/Shia split in Islam. *Islam for Today.* Retrieved from http://www.islamfortoday.com /shia.htm

[13]as-Siba'i, M. (n.d.). Introduction to the Sunnah and its position in the Islamic law. Retrieved from http://www.islaam.com/Article.aspx?id=240

Hence, there is no one Shariah that is binding on all Muslims around the world. This makes it difficult for Muslims and non-Muslims alike to develop uniform approaches to dealing with Muslims in social, religious, and economic matters.

Some predominantly Muslim countries such as Iran have adopted Shariah law as their legal code. No Western country has adopted Shariah. Some Muslim communities in the United States use Shariah law as a substitute for conventional law in settling disputes between Muslims.

Islamic Finance

Foundational Principles

The practice of Islamic finances is based on foundational principles of Islam. One is the principle of stewardship, which states that everything belongs to *Allah*, and humans are to protect the resources that have been entrusted to them. Another principle is the concept of justice, which starts with *Allah* as a just God who demands justice of all believers.

A third principle is that money is to be a means of exchange, but not a store of value. Muslims are not to make gains just from having money to lend; money must be used for a productive purpose, then gains may be legitimately obtained from that activity. Finally, there is the principle of alms. Giving a loan to another without charging interest is blessed by *Allah*, and it may be that if the borrower defaults on the loan that *Allah* will bless the lender if the loan is forgiven.

Muslims can be involved in economic activity only if the activity is not repugnant to Islamic tradition. For example, work with breweries, casinos, and swine farms is prohibited.

Extent of Islamic Finances

As Islamic consciousness and influence rise, Muslims around the world are establishing institutions which are congruent with Muslim beliefs. There are probably over 500 Islamic banks, other Islamic financial institutions, and Islamic windows now operating in over 40 countries,

Conventional banks are beginning to pay attention to needs of Muslims. Iqbal and Mirakhor (2007) listed such banks as Citibank, the Hong Kong and Shanghai Banking Corporation, Union Bank of Switzerland, the American Express Bank, American Bank, ANX Grindlays, and Chase Manhattan as having established Islamic windows or subsidiaries.

Islamic Markets, Indices, and Ratings

Another reason why today's businessperson should be acquaintted with Islam and Islamic financial practices is the growth of markets for dealing in Shariah-approved stocks, bonds, and financial instruments. Islamic bonds are known by the Arabic name *sukuk*, which will be described more fully below. Islamic funds are traded on many conventional stock markets. Dow Jones has a bundle of indices known as the Dow Jones Islamic Market Indexes.[14][15]

Research, Financial Organizations, Degrees, and Certifications

Many research and industry organizations have been established which guide the industry in the development of new Shariah-compliant financial services. Among such organizations are the Islamic Development Bank (Saudi Arabia), the Islamic Financial Services Board (Malaysia), the International Association of Islamic Banks (Saudi Arabia), the International Center for Research in Islamic Economics (Saudi Arabia), and the International Institute for Banking and Islamic Economics (Cyprus).

The Accounting and Auditing Organization for Islamic Financial Institutions (AAOIFI), based in Bahrain, is developing and publishing Shariah standards for Islamic banks in both Arabic and English.
The AAOIFI is the sponsoring organization for a professional certification program similar to the Certified Public Accountant certification available in the United States. The Certified Islamic Public Accounting (CIPA) program is now recognized by such banks and organizations as the Central Bank of Egypt and Deloitte & Touche (AAOIFI, 2010).[16]

Degrees in Islamic Finance are available in Malaysia, Indonesia, Australia, and Hong Kong.

---

[14]Dow Jones. (2007, February 16). Dow Jones Islamic market indexes. Retrieved from: http://www.djindexes.com/indsidx/downloads/brochure_info/Islamicbroch.pdf

[15]Dow Jones Islamic. (2008). Dow Jones Islamic Market Indexes. Retrieved from http://www.djindexes.com/mdsidx/?event=showIslamicOverView

[16]AAOIFI. (2010). Accounting and Auditing Organization for Islamic Financial Institutions. Retrieved from http://www.aaoifi.com

Shariah-Based Differences in Islamic Economic Activities

Rules for conducting Islamic approved business are found in the Shariah. The form and substance of every economic activity such as lending money, buying and selling, contract law, insurance, buying on credit, use of mortgages, and money markets must all comply with general concepts of stewardship and justice as well as specific rules of the Shariah.[17]

Most economic activities in Islamic financial institutions carry a name derived from Arabic language. This ties the activity to Shariah and emphasizes that the activity is Shariah compliant (El-Gamal, 2006, p. 18).[18] Each Islamic financial institution has a Shariah board composed of financial and Islamic experts who rule on the compliance of the activities in which the institution engages. Since different Islamic traditions have different Shariahs, what is permitted in one institution may not be permitted in another. Unfortunately, there are not many Muslims who are knowledgeable both about banking and Islam who can serve as experts. Thus, many such experts serve on multiple Shariah boards, which may lead to a conflict of interest (Iqbal & Mirakhor, 2007, p. 115).[19]

Riba and Gharar

Two main ways in which Islamic finance differs from conventional finance are the prohibitions against *riba* and *gharar*. Loosely speaking, riba may be identified as "interest." The great majority of Islamic scholars accept that interest at any level is prohibited. In order to avoid riba, Islamic institutions have developed many products that allow uses to avoid riba; examples are given below.

"Although the word [gharar] itself is not mentioned in the Koran, etymologically related words, meaning deception or delusion are. It is however in a number of Hadiths that gharar is condemned" (Warde, 2000, p. 59). Gharar comes in several forms, one of which is "the sale of probable items whose existence or characteristics are not certain, the risky nature of which makes the transaction akin to gambling" (El-Gamal, 2006, p. 58). "Generally speaking, gharar encompasses some

---

[17]Platt, G. (2007). Shariah-compliant corporate finance forges ahead.

[18]El-Gamal, M.A. (2006). *Islamic finance: Law, economics, and practice.* New York: Cambridge.

[19]Iqbal, Z., & Mirakhor, A. (2007). *An introduction to Islamic finance: Theory and practice.* Singapore: Wiley.

forms of incomplete information and/or deception, as well as risk and uncertainty intrinsic to the objects of contract" (p. 58).

As Warde pointed out, *gharar* is not the same concept as risk. "Islam does not even advocate the avoidance of risk. Indeed, incurring commercial risk is approved, even encouraged, provided it is equitably shared. More accurately, gharar refers to aleatory transactions, that is, transactions conditioned on uncertain events" (Warde, 2000, p. 59).[20] Warde gave several examples of activities that are prohibited as gharar. Prohibited are: buying fish that are still in the sea, buying in advance the off-spring that is to come from the stud service of a horse, buying in advance what is in the womb of a cow, purchasing food before it has been weighed, and selling food before having possession of it (p. 60).

Another interpretation of the prohibition is that it prohibits unbundled risk and credit, but not bundled risk and credit. For example, one could buy a cow and its unborn calf, but not just the unborn calf. According to this interpretation, it would be acceptable to buy a warranty on a physical good as part of the sale price.

Our attention now turns to seven Shariah-compliant economic activities, *mudarabah, musharakah, sukut, murabahah, ijara*, Islamic insurance, and credit cards. These descriptions will give the reader further insight into Islamic financial activities.

Mudarabah

A *mudarabah* is an agreement which brings together an agent with capital to invest (*rabbul-mal*) with another agent (*mudarib*) who has managerial skills to form a partnership to conduct a business enterprise. An agreement is made between the rabbul-mal and the mudarib as to sharing of profits. The rabbul-mal bears all losses unless there is negligence, malfeasance, or misconduct on the part of the mudarib (Iqbal & Mirakhor, 2007, p xi). Normally the rabbul-mal is a silent partner and leaves the running of the business to the mudarib. The mudarabah may be limited or unlimited. The way profits are to be shared is determined at the beginning of the mudarabah. Profits cannot be shared until the rabbul-mal has retrieved his original investment.

---

[20]Warde, I. (2000). *Islamic finance in the global economy.* Edinburgh: Edinburgh University.

Musharakah

A *musharakah* agreement is similar to a mudarabah agreement. "It is in effect a joint-venture agreement whereby the bank enters into a partnership with a client in which both share the equity capital, and sometimes the management, of a project or deal" (Warde, 2000, p. 136). The financier may also be any natural or juridic person. In recent years the use of musharakah contracts has increased significantly, for it appears that in practice musharakah contracts are quite suitable for long term financing.

Sukuk

The word *Sukuk* is the plural of the Arabic word *Suku*. As described above in the discussion of riba, selling bonds purely on the basis of money alone would not be acceptable. However, it is possible to make gains off a real asset. Thus, to introduce a Shariah-compliant bond, there must be an asset or bundle of assets to which the bond is tied. The buyer of the bond buys a share in the ownership of the asset and benefits from the gains or losses of that asset. A suku becomes Shariah-compliant through the use of mudarabah, described above.

Murabahah

Murabahah refers to a particular type of contract which is used to purchase goods on credit. If economic person A, natural or juridic, desires to purchase a product from person B, A and B agree on a price. Person A then approaches a financier F, which may be a bank, for funds. A agrees to purchase from F the item at the price agreed upon with B, together with a mark-up to the price of the product. Person A and financier F agree on terms including the mark-up to the cost of the product and on a repayment schedule. Financier F then purchases the product from B, then allows A to use the product. A pays for the privilege by paying the financier either on installments or with a lump-sum payment at some specific time in the future. The product itself may serve as collateral for the transaction. A murabahah contract is not a loan, for the financier actually purchases a good which is then used by the entrepreneur to conduct a business activity.

Ijara

An *ijara* agreement is used when a natural or juridical person wants to lease an asset from another person. The lessee receives possession, but not ownership, of the asset which is then used by the lessee in Shariah-approved activities to gain the usufruct arising from possession of the asset (Kettell, 2010).[21] In an ijara agreement the lessor is responsible for maintaining the asset. If insurance coverage is desired, the lessor is responsible for providing for that insurance. The lessor may raise the rental amount to cover insurance costs, but that must be agreed to at the time the agreement is made. With respect to maintenance of the asset, by agreement, the lessor may transfer that responsibility to the lessee who will perform the maintenance for a fee.

Islamic Insurance

For centuries insurance has been *verboten* to Muslims. Insurance was viewed as having elements of gambling, betting, and gharar. In recent years the prohibitions and the stigma associated with insurance have gradually diminished, even those stigmas associated with betting against *Allah*. Now it is even viewed by some as good planning and good risk mitigation, and taking care of one's heirs. To make insu-rance acceptable, changes are typically made in the legal relationship between the premium payer and the insurance company. A mudarabah contract is usually used between the buyer of insurance and the company. This allows the buyers to "become partners in the insurance company and thus be entitled to a share in the profits and losses of the company" (Warde, 2000, p. 148).

Credit Cards

For many years credit cards were not permitted for practicing Muslims. That has changed in recent years as Islamic banks are starting to issue such cards. Since riba cannot be charged, other arrangements have to be made. It may be that cardholders repay their borrowings by installment, but no interest is paid. Another option is that the card is actually a debit card. A third option is a prepaid card.

Critique of the Islamic System

Islamic finance is certainly alive and well in the Muslim world and elsewhere. The number of Islamic financial institutions is growing, and the ability of Muslim institutions to serve the Muslim public is steadily increasing. There is no doubt that Islamic financial institutions will increasingly be accepted by the non-Muslim world and will be accepted as full partners in the world economic system. Neverthe-

---

[21]Kettel, B. (2010). *Islamic finance in a nutshell.* West Susses, UK: Wiley.

less, there are several impediments that are hindering the growth of Islamic financial institutions and practices.

First is the lack of universal agreement whether the *Quaran* is against interest or just against usury. Second is the lack of uniformity among Islamic institutions as to which financial vehicles are Shariah-compliant.

Third, there is a lack of sufficiently trained Shariah scholars to serve on all the boards that are needed in Islamic institutions around the world (Hawser, 2008, p. 6).[22] The lack of uniform rules makes it difficult if not impossible to develop regulatory systems for Islamic institutions in a country (O'Neill, 2008).[23] Further, the lack of uniform rules makes it difficult to establish performance benchmarks that apply across the industry (Henry, 2004).[24] However, in countries with regulatory systems that apply to conventional institutions, the Islamic institutions have to meet the conventional regulatory requirements and Islamic rules, thus placing the Islamic institutions in double jeopardy.

Fourth, there is the matter of cost. For many products more steps are often required to accomplish a given financial task. These extra steps take more time and cost more than completing the same task in conventional financial entities. This additional cost has been called the "Islamic premium." While some Muslims may be willing to pay slightly more to be Shariah-compliant, the additional cost still is a hindrance to growth.

The fifth, and not the least, problem is that many of the steps in executing Shariah-compliant financial activities are viewed as a subterfuge to keep from paying riba. From the perspective of the client, the total cost of the service is almost exactly what they would pay if they had to pay interest.

Sixth, Islamic financial practices will not blossom until they are fully accepted in the United States, while it is known that there is some opposition to the introduction of Islamic financial practices in the United States.

---

[22]Hawser, C.M. (2008). UK addresses Islamic finance skills gap. Global finance, 22(1), 6.

[23]O'Neill, D. (February 2008). Next step: Build a regulatory framework. *Euromoney*, 39(466), 122-123. Retrieved from http://web.ebscohost.com/ehost/detail?vid=5&hid=102&sid=a5386aaf-e19e-43c7-83f9-ceaf72ed248c%40sessionmgr8

[24]Henry, C. M. (2004). Financial performance of Islamic *versus* conventional banks. In C. M. Henry & R. Wilson (Eds.), *The politics of Islamic finance* (pp. 104-128). Edinburgh: Edinburgh University Press.

While these criticisms draw a negative picture, not everything is dark. Islamic services are increasing in extent, so that almost any activity that can be done by a conventional bank can be done by a Muslim institution. More conventional services are being ruled as acceptable to Muslims or conventional services are being slightly modified to become acceptable. Also, younger Shariah scholars who are better trained in conventional financial services are entering the scene, and they are more willing to accept conventional approaches as Shariah-compliant (Henry & Wilson, 2004, p. 294).[25] Still, the number of Islamic institutions grow, as more experience is gained, as information is exchanged around the world, and as transparency increases, more regulatory institutions and benchmark indices will come into existence that will increase the trust of the Muslim public which in turn will accelerate the growth of Islamic finance. In sum, the future of Islamic finance is bright.

Conclusion

Islam is growing, as is the influence of Islamic business practices. Businesspersons who work in global business need to understand the beliefs and practices of Islam. Further, they must understand the workings of Shariah-compliant institutions and be familiar with the principal financial vehicles Islamic institutions use to conduct business.

International Joint Ventures

Research shows that over 50% of international joint ventures (IJV) fail. There are a variety of reasons, including: lack of cultural understanding, failure to agree on goals, one partner gets what it wants and exits the IJV, disagreement about management, stealing of intellectual property, and poor contracts.

To help protect against IJV failure, entities entering into a joint venture agreement need to write a good contract. Principal topics that should be covered include;

1. Name of joint venture, legal structure, corporate address.

---

[25]Henry, C. M, & Wilson, R. (2004). Conclusion. In C. M. Henry & R. Wilson (Eds.), *The politics of Islamic finance* (pp. 286-295). Edinburgh: Edinburgh University Press.

*this paper is a shortened version of the paper: Dunn, S. L., & Galloway, R. R. (2011). Islam, Islamic Finance, and Christianity. Journal of Biblical Integration in Business. 14(1).

2. Legal jurisdiction and law

3. Joint venture duration.

4. Currency, spread of distribution, amount invested by each party

5. How much each entity invests, and the form of those investments

6. Management control and appointment of managers

7. Board control and appointment of board members

8. Accounting standards

9. Responsibilities of founding entities

10. Intellectual property transfer

11. Taxes

12. Finance control

13. Policies about projects

14. Policies about construction.

15. Scope of production

16. Scale of production

17. Marketing issues

18. Labor management

19. Dispute resolution

20. Breach of contract policies

21. Force majeure

22. Asset disposal on close of IJV

23. Miscellaneous concerns

24. Amendments to agreement

25. Effective start date of IJV

After the IJV is up and running, each parent corporation will need to give considerable management attention to the IJV to assure the IJV meets its stated goals.

Outsourcing and Offshoring

Outsourcing and offshoring are two terms that often get confused. Politicians often use the terms incorrectly when trying to make a point about jobs being taken overseas.

Outsourcing can be either domestic or international. A company A which outsources takes part of its value stream and turns it over to another company B. The activity is turned over to Company B because B is able to conduct that activity better, faster, and/or cheaper than company A. Company B may be domestic to company A, or it may be a foreign company.

A company should study its value stream and map out each segment of the stream. Each segment should be studied with respect to its inputs, outputs, time required, costs, and profits. Best practices and competitors should be identified. The company should then decide whether to maintain that segment inside or outsource that segment to another company which may provide higher quality, reduced costs, or shorter production time.[26]

Offshoring is outsourcing to a company in a foreign country. The foreign country may be far away (farsourcing) or near (nearsourcing). Additional considerations come into play when offshoring. In addition to the usual considerations for outsourcing, other matters such as management control, quality assurance, transportation costs and time, insurance, and tariffs must be considered. It may be that the additional requirements for going foreign eat up the cost savings that the foreign production narrowly conceived would produce.

Lots of people complain about jobs going overseas, but they sometimes talk about the matter in terms of outsourcing. They should be more specific and talk about offshoring or foreign outsourcing. Offshoring and outsourcing may or may not be good for the economy. Each instance has to be considered on its own merits.

Outsourcing: Should We?

The big question for the day: Should we outsource part of our value stream to some other company? Second question: Should we offshore part of our value stream?

These questions are fundamental strategic questions for a company. The decisions to outsource and offshore represent big risks to the company. If a firm outsources an activity, then later decides to inhouse that activity, it may take several years to recover. For one thing, outsourcing an activity may cause the firm to lose the expertise needed to conduct that activity; the expertise will have to be rebuilt.

---

[26]Koch, R. (2011). *Strategy: How to Create, Pursue, and Deliver a Winning Strategy* (4th Ed.). New York, NY: Prentice-Hall.

Before making a decision to outsource, a firm should make several studies and take several actions. The most fundamental is that the firm has to understand itself. Every aspect of its value stream must be scrutinized in depth with a SWOT analysis on each part. Granular financial analysis must be conducted on each part for the firm to truly understand what its costs and revenues are for each element of its value stream.

This calls for detailed documentation of each part. Attempts should be made to make tacit knowledge explicit. Moving tacit knowledge to explicit knowledge may be helped by collecting anecdotes and stories about the work. Knowledge held in people's heads must be reduced to writing as much as possible.

If it is determined, after strict analysis, that an activity may be considered for outsourcing, then efforts must be redoubled to make sure that each such activity is understood by the firm, that it is well documented, and the activity can be explained in detail to a firm to which the activity may be outsourced. All details of the activity and how it fits into budgets and calendars must be documented.

Special attention must be given to understanding quality and quality control. The firm must be able to describe in detail the measures and metrics that will be used to assess high quality attainment.

Outsourcing will require some new activities for the outsourcing firm. One is communication with the receiving firm. How is communication to be carried on? Who is to do the communicating? Who has authority at the outsourcing firm to call into question quality control matters? Who makes decisions about redress of calendar and quality issues?

Another activity will be placement of personnel and travel of personnel between the outsourcing and receiving firms. Will the outsourcing firm place some of its people on site in the receiving firm? Will the receiving firm place some of its personnel in the outsourcing firm?

Another area to consider is information linkages between the two firms. How much access to each other's information will be given? Will a third firm need to be engaged to conduct the IT communication activities?

In recent years offshoring of manufacturing has been one of the main ways companies have outsourced. The differences in wages between U.S. wages and wages in other countries have been so pronounced that many companies have enjoyed significant labor savings, making the offshoring venture quite lucrative. However, some of that has changed in recent years as wages have risen in many other countries, so the differential is not so great. Further, as automation improves many of the jobs formerly done by people can be done by machines, so manufacturing may not need to be taken off shore at all. At the time of this writing, the estimated cost differential between mainland China and the U.S. is estimated to be about 10 cents on the dollar in favor of China. This differential may be eaten up, however, by increased transportation and other costs incurred when manufacturing abroad.

If physical product is being produced by the receiving company, how will the product be moved? All aspects of supply chain management will need to be factored into the discussions. Insurance, legal ownership, and movement of funds are just a few of the matters to be considered.

This list goes on and on. Eventually a contract needs to be written for the benefit of all parties to the transaction. The contract needs to be written very carefully so that both sides can be protected. In general the contract should have a sunset clause to bring the relationship to a close. There must be provisions for breaking the relationship if the target goals are not met.

Developing a good contract is one of the most important aspects of the outsourcing project. Outsourcers should get a good attorney who has experience, someone who can project ahead all the necessary provisions that need to go into the contract. Outsourcers should not lean to their own understanding, but should get an expert to help protect the firm from trouble downstream.

Corporate Language Choice

According to the web site *ethnologue.com* the following numbers of people are estimated to speak the listed language as their first language:

Chinese (several dialects)	.05B
English	.51B
Hindi	50B
Spanish	.42B
Russian	.26B
Arabic	.23B
German	.23B

According to the internet site *internetworldstats.com* in 2015 the top ten languages used on the Internet were:

English	801M
Chinese	649M
Spanish	222M
Arabic	137M
Portuguese	122M
Japanese	110M
Russian	88M
German	82M
French	79M
Malaysian	76M

The six official languages of the United Nations are: English, Chinese, Spanish, Arabic, French, and Russian.

How does that all apply to you? First, if your firm is a domestic firm with no intent to globalize and with no direct connections to the outside world, this information may just be interesting. But if your firm has international interests, then language choice and use should be part of your strategic planning.

Here is a list of questions you might ask about language use in your company.

1. Is there a single official language for the firm? If not officially adopted, is there a language which is the de facto language for your firm?
2. What is (are) the language(s) spoken at your international headquarters?
3. Consider senior management. Can a person be a member of senior management without speaking the de facto or official language?
4. What about your expatriates? Are they expected to learn and speak the language of the countries to which they are assigned?
5. What about your leaders in other countries? Are they expected to learn the official or de facto official language of the firm?
6. What about inpatriates? Are they expected to learn the official or de facto official language?

7. Are leaders in countries other than the headquarters countries who don't speak the official language retarded in their leadership opportunities?

Language choice is one of many aspects of culture that a firm needs to consciously adopt. *Remember, all aspects of culture should be determined by the firm's strategic plan.*

Selling to the Base of the Pyramid

There are approximately 7.3 billion people in the world. Unfortunately, many of these people are very poor and live at subsistence levels. According to Peng, about 5 billion people make less than $2000 per year. Unfortunately, these people have until recently been essentially ignored by multinational corporations. It was viewed that these people had to spend all their incomes just to survive; there was little or no disposable income to buy products sold by the multinationals.[27]

Fortunately, that view is gradually changing. It turns out that many of the people at the base of the pyramid do have some disposable income. While money is hard to access, people at the base use bartering, living off the land, and pooling of incomes to provide for basic necessities. This often leaves small amounts of money available to spend on items that are not absolute necessities.[28]

One good example of selling to the base is the cell-phone industry. In many places around the world the very poor have purchased a cell phone and service, and use them to enhance the quality of their lives. These same people could not have afforded landline phones, even if the landline phones were available. But cell phones are so inexpensive, the technology is so easy to use, and there are so many applications in the lives of the buyers, that millions of people who live at the base of the economy have acquired cell phones.

This example illustrates that if a company can sell just a little into a 5 billion person market, there are profits to make. Companies can sell in large quantities, at very low prices.

There is now evidence to believe that people at the base are influenced by the same type of marketing, and are concerned about product quality, as are more affluent people. Companies which want to sell to the base must do their market research, establish reasonable prices for the target market, and produce products that are of appro-

[27]Peng, M.W. (2013). *Global*. Mason, OH: South-Western.
[28]Prahalad, C.K. (2006). *The Fortune at the Bottom of the Pyramid*. Upper Saddle River, NJ: Pearson Education.

priate quality, and be prepared to take a long term perspective on success.

The marketing processes used to sell in affluent countries will most likely not work in getting to the people at the base. Marketing will need to be tailored to the target audience. Because there is so little profit made on each sale, all other costs, particularly distribution costs, must be minimized. While people at the base can appreciate technologies very well, the items sold must not be too sophisticated technologically.

Research has shown that there is often a poverty penalty paid by people at the base of the pyramid. Borrowing money may require very high interest rates. Buying goods may be more expensive because of intermediaries who raise prices more than would be raised in more affluent regions. When large companies determine to sell to the base, they need to influence intermediaries to reduce their costs and prices to allow the goods and services to get to the end customers.

The bottom line is: There is lot of money to be made from selling to the base of the pyramid.

Saving Face

A manager who desires to practice successfully in another culture must understand the worldview underpinnings of that culture. An extremely important concept in most societies around the world is the concept of face. By face, we mean a person's self- and public image in a social context. Face is similar to reputation or status in a society. A person has a good face if he or she is behaving according to the norms of and expectations for that person's position in society.

Face can be maintained, reduced or enhanced. One must be concerned about one's own face, but also about others' faces. Part of preserving and enhancing one's own face is preserving and enhancing the faces of the other. Giving honor and prestige to another is generally viewed as face-enhancing behavior.

Face-saving measures are actions, behaviors, or speeches that rebuff a future loss of face. Face restoration measures are actions, behaviors, or speech that restore damage that has happened in the past. Face giving behavior enhances the honor of another. Face assertive behavior involves stating one's needs in an honorable way while taking into account the face needs of the other party. Facework involves the methods one uses to enhance, maintain, or cause loss of self-face and another's face. In social interactions two face processes are going on simultaneously, one of which is face preserving and one is face honoring. Both parties in the social interaction engage in both processes.

Generally, face is more important in cultures where power distance is high. Also, face is generally more important in collectivist cultures than in individualist societies. Broadly speaking, about two-thirds of the world's people live in collectivist societies. In those cultures, face must be preserved at all costs.

Individuals in collectivist cultures who violate social norms are likely to feel shame. Shame is a social concept; it exists in relationship to the social context. This is contrasted with guilt, which is more likely to be felt by persons in individualistic societies who violate social norms. An individual may feel guilt whether his or her infraction is discovered or not. Shame will not occur unless another knows about the infraction.

Conflict resolution styles are tied to cultural orientations. Persons from individualist countries have a higher self-face and lower other-face orientation. Persons from collectivist cultures have a more balanced view of self- and other-face orientation and tend to use conflict and negotiation styles that preserve self-face and other-face.

Two individuals who desire to create a common identity, such as in marriage, create a new face, the face of the two together. In most cultures there are public rituals the two will go through to establish the face in the public. The joint face subsumes the individual faces. Similarly, when two individuals break their relationship the joint face is dissolved and the individual faces become dominant. In some societies there are public rituals for the dissolution. Often the disengagement from the intimate relationship can be exceptionally face threatening.

In most high context societies, business cannot fully be carried on between individuals until a personal relationship has been developed. The relationship, the face, is between the individuals, not the companies they represent.

Maintenance of relationships and face is generally more important than the matter of truth, where one defines truth as statements that correspond to reality. Telling something that is true that causes a break in relationship may not be honorable and may reduce harmony in the relationship.

Different high-face cultures have variations on the way face is conducted. In Chinese society, for example, indirectness is prized in communication. People do not want to publicly confront each other, for this might interrupt a harmonious relationship. Rather than saying "no" to a request, a Chinese businessperson might say "it may be inconvenient" or "there are some difficulties." There is much fear of public embarrassment, with an unwillingness to embarrass other people. Owning up to a mistake in public amounts to losing face.

In Chinese culture the ultimate nightmare is loss of face. In business negotiations, in order to avoid loss of face, the Chinese negotiator will make every attempt to reduce uncertainty. Typically, the negotiator will attempt to find out early and in advance if there are non-negotiables. If there is too much opportunity for loss of dignity, the Chinese negotiator may break off the negotiations.

Likewise, in Japanese culture, Japanese negotiators will be highly concerned about failure. They will tend to gather as much information as possible so they have a deep understanding of the situation and can construct negotiations that may be acceptable. All is done to prevent loss of face. In the homeland, failure in school causes much loss of face for males.

In Latin American cultures, maintaining one's personal, family, company, and national honor and dignity are extremely important. Good business relationships emphasize *simpatia* (kindness), *confianza* (trust), *respeto* (dignity) and *personalismo* (interpersonal warmth). Letter writing and face-to-face negotiations must be conducted in ways that will portray these values so that personal relationships may be enhanced and face maintained.

In face-valuing cultures, a person's name is very important. In some ways it serves as the person's brand. Because of the importance of names, they should be used carefully, correctly, and with reverence. One should not make jokes using a person's name, or the family, company, or national name. The family name is sacrosanct.

In face-valuing cultures, the use of business cards is often ritualized. The business card carries the name of the businessperson, and must be treated with the respect given to the businessperson. Treat the business card with respect. Generally give and receive it with both hands. Do not grab it and stick it in a pocket, but study it, and keep it on the table while negotiations are going on. When closing the negotiating session, put the business card in a card carrier and put the carrier in a pocket near your heart.

If you are having a dinner with a host, you do not want to embarrass the host by refusing to eat or drink what is put before you. If you have scruples or religious prohibitions about a food or drink, or if there are health reasons why you cannot partake, make sure your host knows that in advance so the host can make adjustments in advance and there is no public humiliation of the host.

In summary, in working with persons from high context societies, treat them with high respect and work hard to not provide any hint of embarrassment to them.

Classifying Cultures

When one engages with a businessperson from another culture, one needs to learn as much as possible about the individual and about the world in which he or she lives and works. One can find much information in books and on the Internet about a particular culture. It behooves one to make a study in advance before meeting that businessperson and beginning a relationship.

Over the years there have been many studies of countries and cultures with an attempt to draw general notions of the nature of the country cultures. Categorization systems have been developed which promote understanding of a country's culture and the cultural family to which the country belongs.

It should be pointed out that generalizations about a culture may not apply to a particular individual in the culture. The generalization may apply to a majority of the people in the culture, but the attribute under discussion may apply more or less to a given individual.

One broad way to classify a culture is to determine whether it is a *high context* or *low context* culture. High context cultures are characterized by: high importance of personal relationships, hierarchical personal relationships, person oriented rather than task oriented, long term perspectives, and status comes from family or position in society. Low context cultures are characterized by: low importance of personal relationships, egalitarian, task-oriented rather than person-oriented, short term perspectives, and status comes from personal accomplishment.

Cultures may be categorized by the values represented in the culture. For example, values characteristic of the United States would be represented by such words as: equality, individualism, competition, independence, directness, and efficiency. In contrast, key values in Japan would be represented by: cooperation, harmony, belonging, indirectness, collectiveness, age/seniority, and patience.

Cultures may also be described by listing principal characteristics of the people in the cultures. One of the more famous systems is the one developed by Geert Hofstede, who described four, later raised to six, characteristics of a culture. The six categories are:

Power Distance	Uncertainty Avoidance
Individualism	Long Term Orientation
Masculinity	Indulgence vs Restraint

For each of these characteristics an index was developed which represents how the people of a given culture relate to the characteristic. The index is a number from 1 to 100 which numerically describes the culture's placement with respect to the category.

Power Distance assesses the degree of equality or inequality among people in the society. A high index number means there is a great inequality of power and wealth. Mexico has an index number of 81 and Great Britain has a 35.

Individualism deals with the manner the society treats individuals and collective achievement and interpersonal relationships. A high index number means the society places a strong emphasis on individualism. Canada has an 80 and South Korea an 18.

Masculinity considers the degree of gender differentiation in the society. A high index number means there is much gender differentiation, with males dominating the power structure. Japan has a 95 and Chile has a 28.

Uncertainty avoidance considers the tolerance for uncertainty and ambiguity. A high index number indicates the country has a low tolerance for uncertainty and ambiguity. Chile has an 86 and Great Britain has a 35.

Long term orientation considers the degree the society embraces long-term devotion to traditional values. A high index number indicates the country values long-term commitments and respect for tradition. South Korea has a 75 and Canada has a 23.

Indulgence vs. constraint measures the tendency to allow relatively free gratification of basic and natural human desires related to enjoying life and having fun. A high index number indicates the culture supports a relative free gratification of basic and natural human desires. Mexico has a 97 and Indonesia has a 38.

Hofstede took his system one step further by observing that countries group together in terms of their principal characteristics. He called these groups "clusters." One cluster he identified was the Latin American Cluster which included Argentina, Chile, Columbia, Peru, and Venezuela. The Anglo Cluster included the United States, the United Kingdom, Canada, Ireland, South Africa, and Australia. The Far

Eastern Cluster included the Philippines, Singapore, Taiwan, and Thailand. [Hofstede was not able to study the People's Republic of China (PRC), so index numbers were not available for the PRC].[29]

Another scholar who described cultures was Erin Meyer. He described cultures using such categories as: persuading, leading, hierarchy, power, decision-making, trust, handling disagreement, and time. His book, *The Culture Map*, gives many interesting anecdotes about work and life in various cultures.[30]

World Bank —World Trade Organization International Monetary Fund

Three corporations have significant impact on the way business is conducted around the world. These are the World Bank (WB), the World Trade Organization (WTO), and the International Monetary Fund (IMF). These three corporations arose from or were derived from organizations that were developed at the end of World War II, when the allies attempted to determine what the world economic order would be after the war. The allies did not want the world to fall into the condition that pertained after World War I when the allies demanded a pound of flesh from the Germans and set a course leading to the rise of Hitler and the world-wide depression.

The three corporations have similar organizations. Each is headed by a group of governors who are the principal financial officers of the governments around the world. Each of the organizations have about 175 country members. When votes are held, the members have a number of votes proportional to the sizes of their economics. The United States has the largest number of votes, with about 17% of the voting power.

World Bank Group

The headquarters of the World Bank Group is in Washington, DC. The World Bank Group has about 10,000 employees. The World Bank Group consists of five corporations: the International Bank for Reconstruction and Development (IBRD); the International Development Association (IDA); the International Finance Corporation (IFC); the

[29]Hofstede, G., Hofstede, G.J., & Minkov, M. (2010). *Cultures and organizations: Software of the mind.* New York, NY: McGraw-Hill.
[30]Meyer, E. (2014). *The culture map: Breaking through the invisible boundaries of global business.* New York, NY: Public Affairs.

Multilateral Investment Guarantee Agency (MIGA); and the International Centre for Settlement of Investment Disputes (ICSID). The terminology "the World Bank" refers to two of the five World Bank Group organizations, the IBRD and the IDA.

The World Bank is a bank, which borrows and lends money for worthy causes. It gets funds in financial markets, with bonds and debt securities sold to insurance companies, pension funds, corporations, banks, and individuals, and interest from loans. The WB is the largest external funder of education around the world, and the largest external funder of HIV/AIDS projects. It is one of the largest external funders of health programs. It strongly supports debt relief and international biodiversity projects.

The IBRD's goal is to reduce poverty in middle-income and creditworthy poor countries. The IDA provides interest-free credits to the world's poorest countries. The IFC encourages economic development in the private sector. The MIGA assists foreign investments in developing countries by providing guarantees against certain noncommercial risks such as expropriation, currency inconvertibility, war, and civil disturbances. The ICSID provides facilities for conciliation and arbitration of investment disputes.

Three projects funded by the World Bank in 2015 include: US$27.8M for education and institutional strengthening in Togo; US$8.29B for education in Pakistan; and US$24M for energy sector development in the Hyrgyz Republic.

World Trade Organization

The headquarters of the World Trade Organization is in Geneva, Switzerland. There are about 650 staff members in Geneva. The goal of the WTO is to help trade flow smoothly, freely, fairly, and predictively. It does this by administering trade agreements, acting as a forum for trade negotiations, settling trade disputes, and assisting developing countries in trade policy issues.

The WTO develops policies in multi-year discussions, called rounds. The current round is the Doha round, which began in 2001. It is named for the city where the first meeting was held in the capital of Qatar, Doha. Over the years the WTO has worked to reduce tariffs around the world and promote movement of goods, services, money instruments, and intellectual property. The Doha round has not been completed because of significant disagreements between developed and developing countries over agriculture policy.

International Monetary Fund

The headquarters of the IMF is in Washington, DC, across the street from the WB headquarters. The IMF has about 2500 employees, approximately half of whom are economists.

The goals of the IMF are to promote international monetary cooperation; facilitate expansion and balanced growth of international trade; promote stability in exchange rates; and making resources available to members experiencing balance of payments difficulties. The three main areas of IMF assistance are: Financial Assistance, which involves providing credits and loans to member countries with balance of trade problems; Surveillance, which is appraisal of each member countries' exchange rate policies in light of the country's economic policies; and Technical Assistance, which involves giving assistance and training to help countries strengthen their human and institutional capacity.

The IMF often helps countries which get into financial difficulty. Maybe the country can't pay its sovereign debt obligations, or perhaps the country has runaway inflation, or it can't balance its budget. Under certain conditions the IMF may loan or grant funds to the country to help it resolve its financial problems. In recent years the IMF has provided significant aid to Greece, Argentina, Mali, Portugal, Poland, and others.

Importing and Exporting

The United States exports over $2.2 trillion of goods and services each year, and imports $2.7 trillion worth. Both importing and exporting continue to grow as firms globalize. U.S. firms export and import for many reasons, including: the desire for additional markets and customers; seeking other resources such as energy, talent, knowledge, and technology; to minimize risk to level out business cycles; to move elements of the value chain abroad; to work with global customers; to shield impact of global competitors; to exploit economics of scale; and in response to the government.

Once you have decided to export your goods or services, you need to find buyers. There are several sources of information about buyers, such as the Michigan State University Center for International Business and Education Research; the Small Business Administration Office for International Trade; and the U.S. Department of Commerce. Your business sector may have organizations which have information about potential customers. In your personal travel around the world you may come across potential customers. You may attend trade shows to learn about exporting possibilities.

A government organization that helps overseas business is the Overseas Private Investment Corporation. It provides project financing, investment insurance, direct loans, and investor services. It en-courage U.S. business competiveness. It works in over 140 countries.

If you want to sell to a foreign buyer you may travel to that for-eign country with samples of your goods. To get your samples into the country you might consider getting a carnet. Many countries use the carnet approach. The *Admission Temporaire Carnet* (ATA Carnet) is a customs document used to get duty-free temporary admission of goods into countries that are signatories to the ATA convention. Fees for the ATA Carnet vary with the value of the goods being carried, but are usually less than $500. A bond must be posted.

By United States law you may not export just anything and every-thing to just anybody. There are persons and countries to which one may not export any U.S. goods or some specific U.S. goods. There are some goods you may not export at all to any country. There are some individuals to whom you may not export any goods. So be very careful to check out your buyers, the countries to which you want to ship, and the specific goods. Most information can be found on the Internet.

The Denied Persons list is a government list giving the names of persons to whom you cannot export or re-export, or participate in any way in any transaction that is subject to Export Administration Regu-lations. Exporting to such persons may result in severe penalties.

Once you have located buyers and have determined it is legal to sell to the buyer, you have to get your goods from your place of busi-ness to their location. There may be several modes of transportation available, including water, air, land or intermodal modes. Pick the method which meets your need in terms of security, speed, and cost.

You will need to pack and mark your goods to protect against breakage, pilferage, moisture and weather. Different goods require different marks on the package, such as custom codes, package num-bers, weight, dimensions, customer and seller codes, port informa-tion, country origin, fragile, and this side up. Typical documents that go with movement of goods include such items as: bills of lading, packing lists, an invoice, marine insurance papers, and certificates of inspection.

You may want to ship by container. There are approximately 20 million containers in use around the world. Approximately 90% of the world's non-bulk cargo moves by container, with about 25% of all container loads originating in China. The largest ships can carry about 15,000 Twenty-Foot Equivalent Container loads. Be sure to get insurance, for an estimated 10,000 containers are lost at sea each year. Information about shipping companies, containers, and rates may be found on the web.

Be very careful about the purchase contracts and all legal conditions for ownership of the goods in transit. Be sure to specify when ownership transfers from seller to buyer. For example, if it is being shipped by cargo ship, does ownership transfer when the good leaves the seller's premises, or when it arrives dockside, or when it crosses the rail of the ship, or when it is off-loaded at the buyer's port, or when it is released from customs, etc? Also, be sure to specify whose insurance applies to the various stages of the trip. In addition, be sure to specify who pays duties that may be assigned to the transaction. Be sure to know in advance what custom amounts will be required and how, when, and where those duties will be paid.

The United States, and many other countries, have Free Trade Zones. These are geographic areas of the country to which goods may be shipped without paying import duties. These goods may be worked on in the zone and shipped out of the zone to that country by paying the applied tariffs on the modified goods, or may be shipped back out of the country without paying import or export duties. Most states of the United States have at least one Free Trade Zone.

Because of the threat of terrorism, the U.S. government has instituted the Container Security Initiative (CSI). The CSI provides for more inspection of containers coming to the United States by pre-screening, by use of detection technologies and tamper-proof containers, and by identification of high-risk containers.

The U.S. government collects information on goods going outside the United States. The standard form is the Shippers Export Declaration (SED). More information about the SED may be found at the following web site: www.export.gov/logistics/eg_main_018116.asp. To keep track of what is going out, the WTO has developed codes for anything that gets shipped. Countries then adapt the code for their own use. The system is called the Harmonized Tariff Schedule. If printed out it would take about 2000 pages.

Once you have a buyer, you need to get paid for your goods or services. There are many options.

You, the seller, may be paid in advance. It may be an open account sale, or a consignment sale. It may involve using letters of credit. Be sure to specify payment methods and protect yourself against non-payment.

Now to some practical advice. If you are not shipping in large quantities, you may want to hire a firm to export your goods for you. These firms such as UPS, or DHL, can take your goods, develop all the paperwork, provide for moving the goods through customs, and ship with little involvement on the part of your company. If, on the other hand, you are a big shipper, you may have your own export office and experts who know all the steps that must be taken to move the goods in a timely and inexpensive way.

If you do export your goods or services, you will find it thrilling to know your products are being used around the globe. Enjoy!

Free Trade Agreements

The United States has free trade agreements with 20 countries. The countries are:

Australia

Bahrain

Canada

Chile

Colombia

Costa Rica

Dominican Republic

El Salvador

Guatemala

Israel

Honduras

Jordan

South Korea

Mexico

Morocco

Nicaragua

Oman

Panama

Peru

Singapore

Two sets of countries are tied to the United States in multilateral trade barriers. These trade agreements are the North American Free Trade Agreement involving Canada, Mexico, and the United States; and the Dominican Republic--Central American Free Trade Agreement involving the Costa Rica, the Dominican Republic El Salvador, Guatemala, Honduras, Nicaragua, and the United States.

At the time of this writing the United States is negotiating two major trade agreements:

The Transatlantic Trade and Investment Partnership with the European Union, and the Trans-Pacific Partnership Agreement and Investment Pact. This latter agreement involves these countries: Australia, Brunei Darussalam, Canada, Chile, Japan, Malaysia, Mexico, New Zealand, Peru, Singapore, and Vietnam.

At one point in the early 90s at the time of the George H.W. Bush administration, there was a desire by many in the U.S. government to create the Free Trade Area of the Americas (FTAA). The dream was to bring all the countries of the Americas under one free trade agreement. This intent was followed up by the Clinton and George W. Bush administrations. However, opposition to the FTAA arose, mainly in key South American countries, so the dream was not realized. Given that the multilateral agreement could not be advanced, the United States continued to develop bilateral agreements or agreements involving a small number of countries.

Many countries around the world have signed Free Trade Agreements with other countries. There are many bilateral agreements and several multilateral agreements. Examples of the latter are the *Mercosur Agreement* in South America, the *East African Community* and *the Southern African Development Community*, and *ASEAN* (the Association of Southeast Asian Nations).

The principal purpose of a Free Trade Agreement is to reduce barriers to trade between the signatory countries. This typically means reduction in ingoing and outgoing tariffs and reduction in not-tariff barriers to trade. In general, once a free trade agreement is signed, tariffs do not move to zero immediately. Rather, tariffs are moved down slowly and carefully so the economics of the countries involved would not suffer.

Toward the North American Common Market

There are five recognized stages of the economic integration of countries. The beginning level is the Trade Agreement. Two countries agree to lower tariffs on selected goods that move between the two countries. The next level is the Free Trade Area. This puts a trade agreement in place with no tariffs between member countries. More than two countries may be involved in a Free Trade Area. The United States is part the North American Free Trade Agreement (NAFTA), which involves the countries of Canada, Mexico, and the United States.[31]

More integration is represented by a Customs Union, which is a Free Trade Area in which the member countries have a common external tariff on goods imported from nonmember countries. The next level is the Common Market, which is a Customs Union where there is free mobility among member countries of the factors of production such as labor and capital. The European Union with its 29 member countries is an example of a Common Market.

Finally, there is Complete Economic Integration, which is a Common Market with common economic policies, common currency (or equivalent), and a common central bank. The European Union does not have complete economic integration; for one thing, there is no common central bank with full economic responsibility for all countries.

Some businesspersons have argued that NAFTA should be upgraded to a Common Market. This would allow the four main factors-goods, money, intellectual property, and people to move freely back and forth across the countries' borders.

It appears most people in the three NAFTA countries would support easier movement of goods, money and money instruments, and intellectual property across the borders. However, there is much resistance to the notion of allowing people to freely cross the borders. As this is written in the midst of the U.S. Presidential election campaign, there is considerable rhetoric to make the laws more stringent about movement of people across the borders, rather than making it easier.

NAFTA took effect on January 1, 1994. The treaty establishing NAFTA called for reduction of tariffs over a period of many years; some tariffs have still not gone to zero, and there is still considerable red

---

[31]Daniels, J., Radebaugh, L., & Sullivan, D. (2011). *International Business: Environments and Operations(13th ed.)*. Boston, MA: Prentice-Hall.

tape about movement of goods around the three countries. It would certainly improve the practice of business if the tariff and non-tariff barriers to the movement of goods, money and money instruments, and intellectual property would be completely removed. The costs for required authorizations, licenses, and non-tariff barriers are substantial and could be reduced significantly.

Objections to the free movement of people across borders typically focus on Mexico. Mexico is a developing country, much poorer than the United States and Canada. Mexicans' principal language is Spanish, not English or French. Mexican cultural values are claimed by some to be quite different from those in the United States and Canada. There are already several million undocumented Mexican citizens in the United States. One report is that on any given day 10% of the population of Mexico is in the United States, legally and illegally. It is argued that if the borders were opened, Mexicans by the millions would flood across the United States' southern border.[32]

These arguments have some validity, but there are also arguments for increasing business with Mexico and opening the borders to people movement. One is the Mexican economy is growing nicely. The International Monetary Fund Forecast, as reported by knoema.com, gives the following predicted percentage changes in real GDP growth:

Year	Percentage Growth
2015	2.31
2016	2.8
2017	3.13
2018	3.22
2019	3.31

Further, the Peso has for several years been relatively stable vis-à-vis the U.S. dollar.

Mexico represents a huge market for U.S. and Canadian goods and services; there are approximately 120 million people in Mexico who are eager and willing to buy products produced in the United States and Canada; there is a growing middle class. This huge market is very close geographically to the United States and Canada.

Mexico is known to have huge deposits of natural resources such as oil and chemicals. Easier access to these natural resource supplies

---

[32]Caplan, B. (2015). Open Borders: The Case. Retrieved from http://openborders.info/double-world-gdp.

would enhance business in the United States and Canada. Further, opening the Mexican economy to U.S. and Canadian investors would permit much economic development in Mexico.

Mexico is rapidly developing into a full-blown democracy. The one-party dictatorship existent in Mexico after the 1917 revolution has been broken; there are now viable political parties at the national level. The rule of law is being enculturated into the life of the people.

At the time of this writing, with the Mexican economy improving, the net movement of Mexicans across the borders is at zero. The speculation that millions of Mexicans would cross an open border is not supported by research nor by analysts speculating on future developments. With the improving economy in Mexico and with the additional Foreign Direct Investment that would be brought to Mexico, the economic incentive to move to the United States would be significantly lessened. Companies moving into Mexico would need workers there. Further, there would be much more movement of Mexican citizens back to Mexico from the United States who would not be trapped by U.S. laws and the difficulties now realized by undocumented Mexicans attempting to cross back into Mexico.

On the other hand, the labor shortages predicted for the United States in the decades ahead would provide incentives for Mexican workers to help fill the available jobs. Some U.S. industries that now having difficulty getting workers would benefit by making it easier for Mexican workers to come to the United States. But they would be coming legally.

Developing a North American Common Market would take at least a decade of work. Many laws and regulations restricting foreign investment would need to be rewritten. Border practices would need to be modified. Companies in all three countries would need to gear up to establish branches in the other countries. Development of joint ventures would take several years to blossom. But the work would be worth it. Some estimates are that the GDPs of the three economies would move up at least 1%-2% above current growth rates each year if the Common Market was to be formed.

In summary, the development of the North American Common Market has much to commend it, with very little downsides. Let's move to enhance our economies by partnering with our near neighbors, to the benefit of us all.

Security and Prosperity Partnership of North America

When it became apparent that the North American Common Market would not move forward with expanded provisions, the leaders of Mexico, Canada, and the United States moved ahead to form the Security and Prosperity Partnership of North America (SPP). In March 2005 the three leaders, Vicente Fox of Mexico, George W. Bush of the United States, and Paul Martin of Canada, met in Texas to sign the partnership agreement. Three later leaders—Harper, Nieto, and Obama—have met on the SPP agenda.

The agreement complements the NAFTA agreement by adding security, foreign policy, and intent to harmonize regulations to the common understandings about economic development of Northern America.

The SPP is not a formal treaty, and hence is not legally binding on the three countries. It might be viewed as a general statement of intent, giving a direction to future economic integration of the three countries.

In the meantime, the United States continues to develop bilateral and multilateral treaties with countries around the world. In recent years the United States has approved trade agreements with Colombia, Panama, South Korea, and the CAFTA-DR (Central American countries and the Dominican Republic) group. The dream of the Free Trade Area of the Americas is still there, but may not be realized for many years to come.

Currency and Exchange Rates

One of the earmarks of a nation is that it has its own currency. In today's world, almost every country has its own unique currency; it is a symbol of sovereignty. Currencies will carry a name given by the country; here are a few:

United States	Dollar
Mexico	Peso
Japan	Yen
Russia	Ruble
South Korea	Won
Canada	Dollar

China	Renminbi (Yuan)
India	Rupee
South Africa	Rand

A country's currency is a commodity. It can be bought and sold. If it can be bought and sold freely it follows the laws of supply and demand.

The rates at which currencies are sold are known as exchange rates. Exchange rates can be found on the Internet---http://www.xe.com/currencyconverter/-and in such newspapers *as The Wall Street Journal*. Exchange rates may be quoted directly or indirectly. For example, suppose the Japanese Yen is trading 100 Yen to the U.S. dollar. That expression is said to be an indirect exchange rate vis-à-vis the U.S. dollar. On the other hand, the exchange rate may be quoted as 1 Yen = $.01; this is a direct quote for the Japanese currency with respect to the U.S. dollar. Note that the direct rate and the indirect rates are reciprocals of each other.

Sometimes a business will want to know what the exchange rate will be 1-month, 3-months, or 6-months ahead. These rates can also be found on the Internet. The current rate is known as the *spot rate*. The predicted rates are the *1-Month Forward Rate*, the *3-Months Forward Rate*, and the *6-Months Forward Rate*.

When you travel to a foreign country you may see a sign like this one in Mexico

WE

BUY SELL

U.S. DOL 11 12

CANADIAN DOLLAR 12   13

From this you know that the shop will buy your U.S. dollars and you will receive 11 Mexican Pesos for each dollar. Also, the shop will sell U.S. dollars for a cost of 12 Mexican Pesos.

If a country attempts to control the value of its currency and not let the value be set on the open market, a black market in the currency may arise. The black market prices will generally better reflect the true value of the currency vis-à-vis other currencies.

Suppose Mexico has fixed exchange rates of Peso vs. the US$, and the official rate is $1=5 Pesos (Buy), 6 Pesos (Sell). Suppose further that the black market rate is US$1= 7 Pesos (Buy), 8 Pesos (Sell). Suppose a tourist takes $10,000 into Mexico, converts on the black market to Pesos and gets 70,000 Pesos. The tourist then spends the tourist spends 30,000 Pesos. On leaving Mexico, the tourist re-converts the remaining 40,000 Pesos on the legal market, and on leaving will have $6,666.

Governments may attempt to maintain the value of their currencies against another major currency or a bundle of currencies. If the exchange rate is fixed, it is said to be *pegged*. If it is allowed to be bought in an open market the currency is said to *float*. A government may choose to peg, then float, then peg, then float as time goes by.

The exchange rate between two countries will impact the balance of trade between the two countries. Suppose the exchange rate between Japan and the United States is 80 Yen = US$1. Suppose Japan sells to the United States 80,000,000,000 Yen worth of goods and the United States sells to Japan $1,000,000,000 worth of goods. Then for each of the countries the balance of trade is even. Now suppose the exchange rate changes to 100 Yen = US$1. Now the trade is unbalanced as the United States earns the equivalent of 100,000,000,000 Yen. There is now a 20,000,000,000 Yen imbalance.

Exchange rates change over time. Factors that impact exchange rates include: Supply and Demand, Purchase Power Parity, Interest Rates, Inflation, and Government Intervention. Government Intervention means the government sets the exchange rate by law. Supply and Demand means that the currencies are being bought and sold on the open market and the market sets the sales prices.

Interest rates cause changes in exchange rates. As a general rule, given equal risk, investment money will tend to move to sites with higher interest rates. As money is invested in the site with higher interest rates, that currency will, in the short run, tend to appreciate in value. In the long run, exchange rates will adjust to equalize interest rate returns.

The Purchase Power Parity reason for exchange rates develops from the general principle that over time, the prices of similar goods and services in all countries should be equal when translated to a common currency, minus friction costs.

With respect to Inflation, if inflation rates differ between countries, then exchange rates will modify to accommodate for inflation. The exchanges rates will change approximately at the percentage change of the difference between inflation rates, with the currency that has the higher inflation being devalued.

Legal Systems

Businesspersons need to know the legal system of each country in which they are doing business. They will then be better able to protect themselves and their business interests in coping with officialdom in those countries. Country legal systems vary considerably, so a person can get into trouble fairly quickly if he/she thinks all countries have legal systems similar to the home country's system.

While each country has its own peculiar law system, there are many similarities among countries. With these similarities it is possible to identify a small number of families of law systems. The country members of each family bear close resemblance to each other. In this essay we examine a few of these families.

Common Law Family

Common law is based on laws passed by the government, by practice and by court decisions, with special focus on court decisions. Whenever a decision is handed down by a judge, that decision becomes part of the accepted law and may be applied in future cases.

The doctrine which espouses the use of previous court decisions is called *stare decisis*. With stare decisis precedents are used extensively in court decisions. As a general rule, judges will follow a previous ruling. There is *vertical stare decisis* and *horizontal stare decisis*. In vertical stare decisis a court uses precedents from a higher court, while in horizontal stare decisis a court will use its own precedents.

In establishing common law practice there is no attempt to consider in advance every illegal action or activity. General laws are laid down, then courts will interpret and apply the law in the context of precedents, other laws, and the country's Constitution.

Common law arose in England over a period of centuries, then was transmitted around the world as England governed its colonies. At this time many of the British Commonwealth countries and the United States—except for the State of Louisiana--practice common law. Included are Canada (except for Quebec), Australia, New Zealand, India, Kenya, and Nigeria.

Civil Law Family

In Civil Law countries the government through its legislation attempts to codify all actions and activities that might be contested in courts. The work of the judges is then to apply the laws in an individual situation. In Civil Law countries there is much less emphasis placed on precedents.

If one examines the law codes of Civil Law countries, the totality of written law will typically be much more voluminous than in Common Law countries, for the Civil Law countries try to think about anything that could go wrong and then have a law to control that situation.

Civil Law arose largely out of Roman Law. It was practiced in the Roman Empire and in its successor countries over the centuries. Most of Continental Europe uses Civil Law, as does most of Africa and Latin America. The Russian Federation's and the Chinese legal systems are tending toward Civil Law.

Religious Law Family

Some countries have a legal system based on religious beliefs and practices. One such family of laws is based in Islam, and the systems of law are known as Sharia Law. Sharia Law is based on four sources. First is the *Quaran*, the holy book of Islam. Second is the *Sunnah*, which is the collection of information as to what Muhammad said, did and permitted to do. Third is the *Hadith*, which are the actual sayings of Muhammad, and fourth are *Fatwas*, which are the opinions of Islamic scholars. Since there are several branches of Islam and there are many Islamic scholars who promulgate Fatwas, there is no one Sharia law; each branch has its own version of Sharia law.

Sharia law is practiced in countries such as Iran and Saudi Arabia. It is also practiced in some States of Nigeria, and in other jurisdictions around the world.

Another religious law is based on Jewish faith. Jewish law is the *Halakhah*, which is based first on the 613 laws *(mitzvots)* that are found in the Torah. In order to avoid violating one of the mitzvots, Jewish rabbis have promulgated *gezeirahs*, which may be viewed as guard fences to keep people away from violating the mitzvots. Next there are the *takkanah*, which is a law given by rabbis. Finally, there are *minhags*, customs that have been around for a long time and have become a law of life.

Mixed Systems

In various countries one will find mixed systems of law. Nigeria has several states in which both customary and Sharia law are practiced. Israel practices customary law and Halakhah. Then there are in many countries communities of faith that practice their religious law among themselves but adhere to the customary law for dealings with the government and with outsiders. Many Orthodox Jews in New York City and in London practice Halakhah. Some Muslim communities in the United States practice Sharia law.

There are other mixed systems that combine civil and common law. Holland and its former colonies in Africa, such as South Africa, Zambia, Namibia, and Botswana have combined systems.

One large country with a mixed system is Canada. All the provinces except Quebec practice Common Law, while Quebec practices Civil Law.

Rule of Law and Rule by Law

In some countries with despotic governments there will typically be a legal system, but the laws can be changed quickly and radically by the government. Whenever the ruling class wants to take some action and the law does not permit it, the ruling class just changes the law and moves ahead with its intended act. This is Rule *by* Law. In a true Rule *of* Law situation the law is fairly stable, and persons and governments are in obedience to the law and must conform to the law's provisions; the regular methods for changing the law must be followed and all are under the law's jurisdiction.

Sources of Information

Below is a list of sources of information about global business practices. The URLs given were active sites as of the date of this writing in late 2015.
Base of the Pyramid
The Guardian. 10 lessons for doing business with base of the pyramid markets.
http://www.theguardian.com/sustainable-business/10-lessons-doing-business-base-of-the-pyramid-markets
Central Intelligence Agency
World Factbook. https://www.cia.gov/library/publications/the-world-factbook/
Consulting Firms
McKinsey & Company. http://www.mckinsey.com
Boston Consulting Group. http://www.bcg.com
Bain & Company. http://www.bain.com
Booz & Company. http://www.booz.com
Deloitte Consulting LLP. http://www.deloitte.com

Monitor Group. http://www.monitor.com
PricewaterhouseCoopers LLP. http://www.pwc.com
IBM Global Business Services.
http://www 935.ibm.com/services/us/gbs
Corporate Social Responsibility
McKinsey Global Survey Results.
http://www.mckinsey.com/insights/corporate_finance
/valuing_corporate_social_responsibility_mckinsey_global_survey_
results
CSR Reputation. http://www.reputationinstitute.com/2015-US-CS
R-RepTrak
Corruption
Corruption Perceptions Index.
 http://www.transparency.org/research/cpi/overview
Countertrade
Global Offset and Countertrade Association. www.globaloffset.org
Country Risk Analysis.
PRS Group. www.prsgroup.com
Customs and Tariffs
U.S. Customs and International Trade Guide. www.lexisnexis.com
United States International Trade Commission.
www.usite.gov/tata/hts/index.htm [Harmonized Tariff
Schedule 2015]
Current Information about Risk Conditions
Overseas Security Advisory Council.
https://www.osac.gov/Pages/Home.aspx
Doing Business
Measuring Business Regulations. World Bank Group.
 http://www.doingbusiness.org/
Expatriate Assignments
The Forum for Expatriate Management.
http://www.centaurmedia.com/portfolio/the-forum-for-expatri-
ate-management
*Journal of Global Mobility. The Home of Expatriate Management Re
search.*
http://www.emeraldinsight.com/journal/jgm
Society for Human Resources Management.
http://www.shrm.org/publications/hrmagazine/editorialcon-
tent/2013/0113/pages/0113execbrief.aspx
General Information
World Trade Press. Store.worldtradepress.com

International Trade. http://www.internationaltrade.co.uk/
Global Trade
   Trade Finance Guide: A Quick Reference for U.S. Exporters. www.amazon.com
International Joint Ventures
   The International Joint-Venture. A Discussion with Professor Paul W. Beamish. *Ivy Business Journal.*
International Joint Ventures Handbook.
   http://www.acc.com/chapters/gny/upload/International_Joi Ventures_Handbook.pdf
Legal and Law
Foreign Corrupt Practices Act. http://www.justice.gov/criminal-fraud /foreign-corrupt-practices-act
   Global Sales and Contact Law. [Book]. Schwenzer, Hachem, & Kee. Oxford University Press.
   International Law & Contracts: The Legal Dimension of
International Trade.
   http://www.internationaltrade.co.uk/articles_print.php?CID=& SCID=&AID=30
Importing and Exporting
   Datamyne. www.datamyne.com/us-import-data
   American Association of Exporters and Importers. www.aaei.org
   Incoterms. www.export.gov
   Electronic Code of Federal Regulations. www.ecfr.gov
   Tariffs and Import Fees.
   www.export.gov/logistics/eg_main_018130.asp
Denied Persons List.
   https://www.bis.doc.gov/index.php/policy-guidance/lists-of-par ties-of -concern/denied-persons-list
   Parties of Concern. https://www.bis.doc.gov/index.php/policy-guidance/lists-of-parties-of-concern
   Exporter's Encyclopaedia. www.amazon.com
   UPS Global Exporting. https://global.ups.com/
Risk Management Insurance
   Marsh. Terrorism and Catastrophe Insurance.
   http://www.shrm.org/publications/hrmagazine/editorialcon-tent/2013/0113/pages/0113execbrief.aspx
   Lloyds of London. https://www.lloyds.com
Shadow Economy
   Hiding in the Shadows: The Growth of the Underground Economy. International Monetary Fund.

http://www.imf.org/external /pubs/ft/issues/issues30

Sources of Funds

International Finance Corporation.

http://www.ifc.org/wps/wcm/connect/corp_ext_content/ifc_external_corporate_site/home

Chapter 2

Target Countries

In this section of the book we will look at several countries in which you may be doing business. These countries are ones that are prominent in international trade with the United States, or they are ones with large Gross National Products.

While working in foreign countries it is very important that the businessperson have a basic understanding of the national culture in which he or she will be working. There should be a good understanding of several specific aspects of the culture, including the following:

National Constitution

Branches of National Government

State or Provincial Geographic Organization

Constitutional Provisions for Business

Operations

Commercial Code

Corporation Organization Options

National and Provincial/State Taxation Rates

Personal Income Rates

Repatriation of Profits

Contract Law

Provisions for Patents, Copyrights, and Trademarks

Specific Laws Related to Your Business Sector

In addition to these aspects of the national culture, the business-person working in the nation should have general knowledge of the history of the nation, its national symbols, and national holidays. Finally, there should be a general understanding of the risks of doing business in the country. This information can be obtained by doing a country risk analysis. (See the essay on Country Risk Analysis).

The following countries are considered: Brazil, Canada, China, India, Japan, Mexico, Nigeria, Russia, and South Africa.

Before considering each of these countries, consider the differences in ease of doing business in these countries. The World Bank Group publishes information about doing business in 189 countries (http://www.doingbusiness,org/rankings). One of the rankings is the Ease of Doing Business Rank. Each country is given a number from 1-189; the higher the number the easier it is to conduct business in the country. Here are the rankings for the countries considered, as well as the United States.

Country Ease of Doing

Business Ranking

United States 7

Canada 14

Japan 34

Mexico 38

Russia 51

South Africa 73

China 84

Brazil 116

India 130

Nigeria 169

It should be pointed out that the author of these essays is not an attorney. The essays are accurate to the best of the author's ability and knowledge. However, the reader is encouraged to engage an attorney in any target country to get the latest and most accurate information about the country and business practices therein.

BRAZIL

The Federative Republic of Brazil (Brazil) came into existence in the early 1800s after separation from Portugal. Brazil's current population is approximately 200 million. By land size it is the fifth largest country after Russia, Canada, the United States, and China. In 2016 the CIA estimated the 2013 Brazilian Gross National Product on a purchase power basis as US$2.422 trillion. The capital is Brasilia. The country is divided into 26 States and a Federal District. The largest city is Sao Paulo with population nearing 20 million. Portuguese is the official language of the country. About 75% of the populations are Roman Catholics, and 15% are Protestants.

Brazil is a member of several trade groups. One is *Mercosur* which involves the countries of Brazil, Argentina, Bolivia, Paraguay, Uruguay and Venezuela, with several other countries as associate members. Brazil is also a member of the *General System of Trade Preferences Among Developing Countries,* the *Latin American Integration Association*, and is a signatory to the *Protocol Relating to Trade Negotiations among Developing Countries.*

The Brazilian government has three branches: executive, legislative, and judicial. The head of state and chief of state is the President, currently Dilma Rousseff. The President is elected by popular vote. The term of office is four years.

The country's legislative branch, the National Congress, is bicameral; the two branches are the Federal Senate and the Chamber of Deputies. The Federal Senate has 81 members, three from each state and the Federal District; each elected for an eight year term. The Chamber of Deputies has 513 members, elected by proportional ballots in the States, for a four-year term of office.

The judicial branch is headed by the Federal Supreme Court whose 11 members are appointed by the President and confirmed by the Federal Senate, with lifetime terms. Also there are the National Council of Justice, the Superior Court of Justice, and various regional Federal courts.

There is a Superior Court of Labor, with 27 justices appointed by the President and approved by the Federal Senate. This court deals with "i. judicial actions arising from labor relations...; ii. judicial actions involving the exercise of the right to strike;...v. conflicts of po-wers between bodies having jurisdiction over labor issues...;" and other matters.

There are many local and national political parties in Brazil. The current President, Dilma Rousseff, is from The Worker's Party.

Brazil is a member of many international organizations, including: the United Nations, the World Bank, the World Trade Organization, and the International Monetary Fund

The current Brazilian Constitution was adopted in 1988 and has been amended several times. The English version of the Constitution with its amendments and additions is approximately 95 pages long. It is divided into nine Titles and 250 Articles. Brazil practices civil law under a *Civil Code* adopted in 2002.

The Constitution begins with the statement that Brazil is a "....legal Democratic State...The fundamental objectives of the Federative Republic of Brazil are: i. to build a free, just and solidary society; ii. to guarantee national development; iii. to eradicate poverty and marginal living conditions and to reduce social and regional inequalities; and iv. to promote the well being of all, without prejudice as to origin, race, sex, color, age, and any other forms of discrimination."

Article 5 of the Brazilian Constitution deals with equality. "All persons are equal before the law, without any distinctive whatsoever, and Brazilians and foreigners resident in Brazil are assured of inviolability of the right of life, liberty, equality, security, and property..."

Article 7 deals with workers' rights. Rights include "i. employment [is] protected against arbitrary dismissal or against dismissal without cause; ii. unemployment insurance...iv. a minimum wage; viii. a thirteenth [monthly] salary...; xii. family allowance paid to each dependent of low-income workers...; xviii. maternity leave without loss of job and of salary, for a period of one hundred and twenty days; xxiii. additional compensation for unhealthy or dangerous work...; xxv. free assistance for children and dependents of up to five years of age, in day-care centers and pre-school facilities; xxviii. work accident insurance...xxxii. prohibition of any distinction between manual, technical, and intellectual labor or between respective professionals."

Article 9 gives workers the right to strike.

Article 145 gives the Federal government and State governments the right to institute taxes, fees, and assessments. Article 153 gives the Federal government the right to institute taxes on imports, exports, income and earnings, industrialized products, various money transactions, and large fortunes.

Article 173 provides for "the legal system of public companies, joint-stock companies and their subsidiary companies engaged in economic activities connected with the production or trading of goods, or with the rendering of services..."

Article 179 provides for simplification of legal requirements and obligations for micro companies and small companies.

Article 196 asserts that "Health is the right of all persons and the duty of the State and is guaranteed by means of social and economic policies..." Further, "The single health system is financed ...with funds from the social security budget...."

Article 208 guarantees "mandatory basic education, free of charge, for every individual from the age of 4 (four) through the age of 17 (seventeen), including the assurance of its free offer to all those who did not have access to it at the proper age;..." Article 209 states that "Teaching is open to private enterprise," on conditions.

Article 215 asserts the "The State ensures a person full exercise of their cultural rights and access to sources of national culture and supports and encourages the appreciation and diffusion of cultural manifestations."

Article 220 deals with Freedom of Communication. "Expression of thought, creation, speech, and information, in any of their forms, processes or media, may not be subject to any restriction..."

The primary enabling legislation which legalizes company practices in Brazil is found in the *Civil Code* and the *Commercial Code*. Recent revisions have eliminated significant sections of the *Commercial Code*; that information is now found in the *Civil Code*.

The law recognizes various types of companies that may be registered. The two principal types are the corporation (SA) and the limited liability company (LTDA). Brazilian law also recognizes associations, foundations, cooperatives, and joint ventures. Trusts are not recognized by law. Brazilian law provides for mergers and acquisitions, provided anti-monopoly laws are not violated.

Corporations may be closely held or publicly held. Publicly held companies must be registered with the Brazilian equivalent of the U.S. Securities and Exchange Commission. Brazilian corporations must have at least two shareholders. There are few publicly held companies in Brazil, around 1000. A management board is mandatory in publicly held corporations and must have at least three members.

The LTDA form is the most used form of business organization in Brazil. It is similar to limited partnerships and limited liability companies in the United States. At least two partners are required to form an LTDA. Over six million businesses in Brazil are small or medium size entities.

Business corporations (SAs) or businesspersons doing business activities must register with the Commercial Registry. Companies which are not SAs must register with the Civil Registry.

Foreign corporations may register in Brazil, subject to few limitations. Foreigners may own buildings in Brazil, with some limitations on obtaining rural real estate. A foreign company may not open branches in Brazil except with special permission and finally receiving Presidential authorization. Foreign companies must have a local representative in Brazil. Foreign enterprises may own domestic firms, with certain exceptions or restrictions. Generally at least two-thirds of employees in any Brazilian company must be Brazilian citizens and two-thirds of total remuneration must go to Brazilians.

Employees are to receive 30 days of vacation after each 12 months of employment and a 13th month of salary. The maximum work week is 44 hours and the working day is limited to 10 hours. Pregnancy leave for mothers is 120 days and five days for fathers. Employers must provide transportation vouchers so employees can have free transportation to work.

There is a free trade zone, the Manaus Free Trade Zone, established to attract business to the Amazon region.

The national government and the States may impose taxes on individuals and business entities. Residents must pay taxes on Brazilian income and foreign income. Non-residents must pay taxes onBrazilian income, but foreign income is not taxable. Brazil has a double-tax treaty with several countries, but not with the United States.

The corporate income tax rate is 15% on net profits. If a company's profits exceed approximately US$151,000 in a year the amount above US$151,000 is taxed at an additional 10% rate. States impose VAT taxes on sale of goods and services. The tax is assigned to all stages of the chain of sales. A typical company may pay about 70% of its net profits to the government, Federal and state.

Dividends earned in Brazil by shareholders living abroad may be repatriated. Dividends from profits are not subject to withholding tax or income tax. Interest may be paid to a foreign lender.

Some reductions in taxes may be realized from government incentives, such as less tax on imported capital goods not available locally, or reduction of taxes on purchase of capital goods by exporting enterprises, or for technological innovation.

The law provides for common contracts as well as many types of specialized contracts. Brazil has adopted many laws and legal practices similar to those commonly practiced in the international community. However, any investor doing business in Brazil is advised to become very familiar with the details of the current Brazilian law, since such details may vary from those of the investor's home country.

Brazil adopted in 2014 the *United Nations Convention on the International Sale of Goods (CISG)*. Also, Brazil is a signatory to several international treaties considering intellectual property rights. Included among these are:

Berne Convention

World Intellectual Property Organization Convention

Trade Related Aspects of Intellectual Property Rights

Paris Convention for the Protection of Industrial Property

World Intellectual Property Organization Convention

Patent Cooperation Treaty (PCT)

Brazil is not a member of the OECD.

Brazilian law provides for protection of intellectual property rights through patents, copyrights, and trademarks. Laws provide protection for company secrets and industrial designs. Also, protection is provided for intellectual property rights related to new agriculture plant varieties.

Patents have a term of 10, 15, or 20 years from the date on which the patent was applied, with the term depending on the patent category. Patents must be capable of being produced or applied in an industrial process.

Copyrights give intellectual property protection to the creators of original works of authorship. The term of a copyright in Brazil is 70 years from the death of the creator. Copyright protection begins at the time of creation of the work. Copyrights are given for an expression of an idea, not the idea itself. Protection begins when the creative work is completed.

Brazilian law provides for the registration and legal protection of trademarks. *The International Classification of Goods and Services* is used in identifying goods and services. Further, Brazil uses the first-to-file system.

It behooves each foreign and domestic entity in Brazil to be a watchdog for its own intellectual property. Company surveillance, swift action, and willingness to press one's position in the courts are necessary to diminish the effects of intellectual property theft.

In developing contracts in Brazil, be sure to have one version of the contract in Portuguese. If the Brazilian courts become involved with the contract, the Portuguese version will be used. Further, it is recommended that contracts in Brazil contain provision for arbitration of disputes. Bringing a matter to court may take many years and involve significant costs.

Doing business in Brazil may take much time working with the red tape, high interest rates, taxes, and labor laws. The additional cost is sometimes known as the *Brazil Cost*. It should be noted that the underground economy of Brazil was estimated by Friedrich Schneider in 2007 for the years 2004/2005 to be 41.8% of the GNP.[33]

Readers are encouraged to determine current Brazilian laws and to engage a Brazilian attorney when doing business in Brazil.

Canada

Canada became a self-governing country in 1867, but remained in close connection with the United Kingdom. Canada has a population of approximately 35 million people. It is the second largest country in the world by land size, being about half the size of Russia and slightly larger than the United States. In 2016 the CIA estimated the 2013 Canadian Gross National Product in 2012 on a purchase power basis as approximately US$1.518 trillion. The country has 10 provinces and three territories. Ottawa is the capital of the nation.[34]

English and French are the two principal languages, with about 60% of the population speaking English and 20% speaking French. About 43% of the population are Catholics, 23% are Protestants, and 2% are Muslims. The urban population is about 80% of the total.

Canada is a parliamentary democracy. Queen Elizabeth II is head of State, who is represented in Canada by the Governor General. The head of government is the Prime Minister, currently Justin Trudeau. The Canadian government has three branches: executive, legislative, and judicial. The party having the majority in the House of Commons normally selects one of its own to be the Prime Minister. The House then recommends that person to the Governor General, who appoints the Prime Minister.

There is a bicameral Parliament consisting of the Senate and the House of Commons. The Senate has 105 seats. The members of the Senate are appointed by the Governor General and may serve until age

---

[33]Schneider, F. (2007). Shadow economies and corruption all over the world: New estimates for 145 countries. *Economics* (2007-2009)

[34]Natural Resources Canada: www.gove.mb.ca Invest in Manitoba: www.gov.mb.ca/jec/invest /busfacts/govt /invest _can_act.html

75. The House of Commons has 308 members who are elected in the provinces and territories for four-year terms.

The judicial branch is headed by the Supreme Court of Canada. Judges are appointed by the Governor General upon the advice of the Prime Minister. There are other national courts, such as the Tax Court of Canada.

There are a few national political parties in Canada. Among them are the Bloc Quebecois, the Conservative Party, the Green Party, and the Liberal Party. The current Prime Minister is from the Liberal Party.

Canada is a member of many international organizations, including: the United Nations, the World Bank, the World Trade Organization, and the International Monetary Fund.

The governing law of Canada consists of several written laws, unwritten customs, traditions, and judicial decisions. The Constitution Act of 1982 transferred control of the Constitution from the UK to Canada. The Constitution may be thought of as a living document which can be modified fairly readily. Canada practices Common Law, except in the Province of Quebec which practices Civil Law.

In addition to national and provincial law, there are also municipal governments. Aboriginal people who live in First Nation areas have different types of governments. Various rights have been recognized for aboriginal people to allow them to maintain traditions and customs.

The *Canadian Bill of Rights* (1960) guarantees basic rights, such as those of life, liberty, security, and property. The *Canadian Human Rights Act* (1977) provides for equality in areas of employment, services, and housing. These acts are supplemented by human rights acts passed at the provincial level. The *Canadian Charter of Rights and Freedoms* guarantees other rights and declares citizen responsibilities.

Among the various rights guaranteed by law are: freedom of religion; freedom of the press; the right to enter or leave the country; the right to live or seek work anywhere in the nation; guarantee of protection of life, liberty and physical and psychological safety; the right to be presumed innocent until proven guilty; guarantee against arbitrary arrest or detainment, guarantee against cruel and unusual punishment; the guarantee that everyone is treated the same before the law regardless of national or ethnic origin, religion, gender, color, age, sexual orientation, or marital status; and the right to use English or French in proceedings in any government court established by Parliament.

The primary enabling legislation which legalizes commercial practices in Canada is found in various *Personal Property Security Acts* and various Laws of Contracts. Canadian contracts must meet five conditions to be legally binding. There must be a purpose; a capacity to perform; a lawful cause; mutual consent; and a written agreement in serious instances. In common-law provinces there must be a consideration.

There are several types of companies in Canada. Whatever the form, the business should be registered with the appropriate government jurisdiction. There are sole proprietorships in which the owner is responsible for all obligations and all profits go to the entrepreneur. Partnerships involve two or more individuals who agree to share obligations and profits according to the partnership agreement. Limited liability partnerships permit one or more of the partners to have limited control of the business with limited responsibilities and profits as stated in the partnership agreement.

Corporations in Canada can be federally charted or provincially chartered. In corporations ownership is transferable, and each owner has limited liability for the actions of the corporation. There may or may not be tax advantages to a corporation as compared to a partnership. A cooperative is another business form available in Canada. In a cooperative the firm is owned by members who belong to some type of association. In the cooperative there is typically limited liability to the members, profit is distributed among the members, and each member has one vote in company decisions.

Foreign investment is normally welcome in Canada. The principal law for investment is the *Investment Canada Act* of 1985. According to this law, foreign investments come in two categories: investments that are reviewable and investments that are subject to notification. Reviewable investments must be approved by the national government. Reviewable investments must pass several tests, including being compatible with national security, not distracting from competition; being compatible with national cultural, economic, and industrial policies; and others.

If a foreigner establishes a new business in Canada or takes over an existing business, the investor must notify the Department of Industry within 30 days. If the investment exceeds thresholds established by the government, the establishment or control may be reviewable. Threshold levels are higher for investors from WTO countries.

A foreign investor's investment or profits may be repatriated without restriction. The Canadian dollar is freely convertible, and there are no exchange controls. According to Natural Resources Canada, "... invested capital can be repatriated tax-free before any withholding taxes are applied."[35]

Corporate tax rates in Canada are typically about 15% for national taxes and average 11% for the provincial taxes. There are no taxes applied to repatriated foreign profits. The national government collects taxes on behalf of the provinces, except for Quebec.

National personal income tax rates are graduated by taxable income levels and range from 15% to 29%, the latter being applied to taxable incomes over $139,000 (approximate). Provincial and territorial personal income tax rates are also graduated by taxable income levels. Provincial and territorial rates range from a low of 4% in Nunavut on the first $42,000 of income to a high of 17.84% on the amount over $129,975 in New Brunswick.

A sales taxation system is used in Canada. Federal sales taxes are charged on most supplies of services and goods in Canada, with the usual exception of some items such as groceries and medical services; the tax rate is currently 5%. In addition to a federal sales tax, some provinces have their own sales tax. Other provinces have blended the two taxes in a Harmonized Sales Tax (HST) system. HST rates may be as high as 15%. Three territories do not have sales taxes. Quebec charges both a goods and services tax and administers the federal tax in the province. For other provinces the system is administered by Federal government.

Canada's tax regime is similar to those in other OECD (Organization for Economic Cooperation and Development) countries. Priority for taxation goes to the country in which the income is made.

Canada has adopted the United Nations Convention on the International Sale of Goods (CISG). Also, Canada is a signatory to several international treaties considering intellectual property rights. Included among these are:

Berne Convention

World Intellectual Property Organization Convention

Paris Convention for the Protection of Industrial Property

World Intellectual Property Organization Convention

Patent Cooperation Treaty (PCT)

---

[35]How Much Lower are Canada's Business Taxes? Taxfoundation.org/blog/how-much-lower-are-Canadas-business-taxes

Budapest Treaty on the International Recognition of the

Deposit of Microorganisms for the Purpose of Patent

Procedure

Rome Convention for the Protection of Performers, Producers of Phonograms

and Broadcasting Organizations

Strasbourg Agreement Concerning the International Patent

Classification

Union for the Protection of New Varieties of

Plants Convention

Canadian law provides for patents, copyrights, and trademarks. Patents give creators a monopoly on their creations for a limited time. The time of monopoly is normally 20 years from the date on which the patent application was filed. Patents go to the first inventor to file an application. Requirements for patentability are novelty, inventiveness, and utility. Not patentable are ideas, a scientific principle, a mathematical theorem, a computer program, or some methods for doing business.

The Copyright Act is the law governing copyrights. Copyrights give intellectual property protection to the creators of original works of authorship, such as musical, dramatic, artistic and literary works. Thus copyright protection would include books, newspapers, computer software, paintings, sculptures, photographs, films, and architectural works.

Normally the creator of the original work is the owner of the copyright. In Canada the creator also has moral rights to the creation. Normally the copyright exists for 50 years from the year of the death of the creator. Copyrights begin upon creation. Copyrights may be licensed or sold, but moral rights may not be licensed or sold.

Canadian law provides for the registration and legal protection of trademarks under the Trademarks Act. Trademarks are used to cover useful or new inventions or a useful improvement to an existing invention. Registration gives trademark protection for 15 years, and is renewable. Some words are not accepted as trademarks, such as: surnames of living individuals or one who has died in the past 30 years; the name of the goods or services that are being described; a geographic location; a denomination; and others.

With this discussion of trademarks we come to the close of our brief review of Canada and the legal framework for Canadian business. It behooves each foreign and domestic entity in Canada to be a watchdog for its own legal status and its intellectual property. Company surveillance, swift action, and willingness to press one's position in the courts are necessary to diminish the risk of getting in legal difficulty.[36]

Readers are encouraged to determine current Canadian laws and to engage a Canadian attorney when doing business in Canada.

CHINA

The People's Republic of China (PRC) came into existence in 1949 when the Chinese communists, under the leadership of Mao Zedong, overthrew the government of Chaing Kai-Shek. China has the largest population in the world with approximately 1.4 billion people. By land size it is the fourth largest in the world after Russia, Canada, and the United States. In 2016 the CIA estimated the 2013 Chinese Gross National Product on a purchase power parity basis as US$13.37 Trillion.

The current Chinese Constitution was adopted in 1982. Amendments were adopted in 1988, 1993, 1999, and 2004. China is a one-party state led by the Chinese Communist Party (CCP). There are other legal, small parties, but they are controlled by the CCP.

The Chinese government has three branches: executive, legislative, and judicial. The head of the executive branch and chief of staff is the President, currently Xi Jinping. The head of government is the Premier, currently Li Keqiang. The President is elected by the National People's Congress for a five year term. The President can serve a maximum of two terms.

The legislative branch, the National People's Congress, is unicameral. There are approximately 3000 members who are elected by local jurisdictions for five year terms. The judicial branch consists of the Supreme People's Court, with judges appointed by the National People's Congress.

The English version of the Constitution with its amendments is 28 pages long. It is divided into four chapters. Chapter III is titled The Structure of the State and contains 138 Articles.

Articles 1-3 state that the PRC is a socialist state, that power belongs to the people, and the government operates under the principle of democratic centralism. Articles 6 and 7 state that the basis of the

---

[36]Current and Emerging Issues: www.parl.gc.ca/content/lop/researchpublications/cei-22-e.htm

Chinese economic system is socialist public ownership of the means of production. The national economy is under the ownership of the entire people of China.

Article 11 allows individual economic activity of urban and rural working people who can own houses, savings, and earned income. Article 15 authorizes a centrally planned economy. Article 17 authorizes collective economic organizations. Article 18 allows foreign entities to invest in China. Article 32 guarantees the lawful rights and interests of foreigners within Chinese territory.

Articles 35 and 36 guarantee freedom of speech, press, assembly, and religion. Article 48 states that women in China have equal rights with men. Article 41 guarantees the rights of whistleblowers.

Amendment 1, passed in 1988, authorizes the private sector of the economy to exist and develop as a complement to the socialist public economy. It further gives authority to individuals and organizations to buy and sell land by legal means.

Amendment 2, adopted in 1993, modifies the philosophy of government and economics to one of socialism with Chinese characteristics, all under the guidance of Marxism-Leninism and Zedong Thought, whose goal is property, democracy, and culture.

Amendment 3, adopted in 1999, restates part of the Preamble. It reaffirms that China is in the primary stages of socialism, that the state economy is the primary economy, and the individual economy is a complement to and major component of the social market economy.

Amendment 4, adopted in 2004, recognizes further changes to the economic philosophy and recognizes the contribution of Deng Xiaoping Theory. It recognizes the rights and interests of the individual and private sectors of the economy. The State protects citizens in their ownership of lawfully earned income, savings, and homes. Citizens may own and inherit private property.

There are two general types of business entities in China, State owned enterprises (SOEs) and private entities. The primary enabling legislation which legalized private business entities in China is the *General Principles of Civil Law (GPCL)*. Three types of private enterprises are identified: limited liability companies, partnership companies, and sole investment companies. A company is a legally recognized person, and must register with the government. Companies may have branches, but they are not separate legal entities. Companies may form subsidiaries which are distinct legal entities. Partnerships are recognized by law.

China allows and encourages foreigners to establish business enterprises in China. Companies established by foreigners are known as Foreign Investment Enterprises (FIEs). There are three main FIE types used: cooperative joint ventures, equity joint ventures, and wholly foreign enterprises. Foreign-China joint ventures must be limited liability companies. One of the most used vehicles for foreign investments in China is a joint venture with a Chinese partner.

Private enterprises may do business with the State. If a business entity needs to obtain land, application must be made to the local political jurisdiction. If land use is granted, the entity will pay a fee.

Foreign enterprises must pay taxes on their business operations in China. One Chinese tax is the Consumption Tax which is typically paid on certain consumer goods. The principal taxing mechanism is the Value Added Tax. When exporting goods, Chinese companies may be able to recover some of the VAT already paid. Foreign-funded enterprises are relieved from import taxes on a wide variety of goods which are used in production.

Chinese law in general and contract law in particular were historically based on Confucian principles and Civil law. China law is now moving closer to a Civil Law system.

The principal law regulating contracts is the *Contract Law of the People's Republic of China*. The law provides for common contracts as well as many types of specialized contracts. China has adopted many laws and legal practices similar to those commonly practiced in the international community. For example China adopted in 1988 the United Nations *Convention on the International Sale of Goods (CISG)*. The CISG is a principal factor in contract law for international enterprises working in China or with Chinese enterprises.

The Intellectual Property Rights laws of China are similar to those of most advanced nations. China has signed several international agreements and treaties involving copyright and intellectual property. Included are the *Berne Convention*, the *Paris Convention for the Protection of Industrial Property*, and the *World Intellectual Property Organization Convention*. The primary law regarding copyrights is the *Copyright Law of the People's Republic of China*. The laws for copyright cover written, oral, artistic, architectural, computer, cinematographic, and other works. China recognizes moral as well as economic rights. Copyrights of Chinese citizens and foreigners who copyright materials in China are covered for 50 years after the death of the author. There are special regulations dealing with computer software. Copyright protection for computer software lasts 25 years.

Patents can be obtained in three categories: invention patents, design patents, and utility models, with terms of 20, 10, and 10 years, respectively. Patents are granted on the first to create, not the first to register. Patents must be registered in China to receive Chinese protection. Foreign companies which have no business office in China cannot directly submit an application for a patent.

Trademarks may be registered in China. Three categories of trademarks are recognized: service trademarks, certification marks, and collective trademarks. A product's generic name cannot be used as a trademark. Well-known foreign trademarks may not be registered in China. China uses a first to file trademark system.

It behooves each foreign and domestic entity in China to be a watchdog for its own intellectual property. Company surveillance, swift action, and willingness to press one's position in the courts are necessary to diminish the effects of property theft.

Readers are encouraged to determine current Chinese laws and to engage a Chinese attorney when doing business in China.

INDIA

The Republic of India (India) came into existence in 1947 after gaining its independence from the United Kingdom. India has a large population of approximately 1.2 billion people. By land size it is about one-third the size of the United States. In 2016 the CIA estimated the 2013 Indian Gross National Product on a purchase power basis as US$4.962 trillion. The country has 28 States and seven union territories.

Each State is headed by a Governor. Some states have a bicameral legislature and some have a unicameral legislature. Territories are administered by the President, who may appoint an administrator as the de facto governor.

The nation and/or its States recognize 22 languages, with English and Hindi being the dominant two. About 80% of the population are Hindu, 15% are Muslim, and 2% each are Christian and Sikh.

The Indian government has three branches: executive, legislative, and judicial. The head of state is the President, currently Pranab Mukherjee. The head of government is the Prime Minister, currently Narendra Modi. The President is elected by an electoral college consisting of the members of both houses of Parliament and members from state legislatures. The term of office is for five years, with no term limits.

The country's legislative branch, the Parliament, consists of two bodies, the Council of State and the House of the People. The Council of State has 245 members, 12 of which are appointed by the President and the remainder elected in staggered elections by the state and territory legislatures. Members serve six-year terms. The House of the People has 545 members, 543 of which are elected by popular vote. Two are appointed by the President. Members serve five-year terms. States and territories have members in the House proportional to their populations.

The judicial branch is headed by the Supreme Court which has one chief justice and 25 associate justices. The justices are appointed by the President and normally serve until age 65.

There are many local and national political parties in India. The current Prime Minister is from the Bharatiya Janata party.

India is a member of many international organizations, including: the United Nations, the World Bank, the World Trade Organization, and the International Monetary Fund.

The current Indian Constitution was adopted in 1950 and has been amended several times. The English version of the Constitution with its amendments and additions is approximately 400 pages long. It is divided into 22 main parts incorporating 395 Articles. In addition there are 12 Schedules and two Appendices. India practices common law based on the British model. There are separate personal conduct laws for Hindus, Muslims, and Christians. The Constitution begins with the statement that India is a Sovereign, Socialist, Secular, Democratic Republic and exists to secure for its citizens justice, liberty, equality, and fraternity.

Articles 14-16 guarantee that the nation will provide equal protection of the laws within the Indian territory and the nation shall not discriminate against any citizen on grounds only of religion, race, caste, sex, or place of birth. Further "there shall be equality of opportunity for all citizens in matters relating to employment or appointment to any office under the State. Article 17 rules out "Untouchability." It is abolished in all forms and practices.

Article 19 guarantees the rights of all citizens to freedom of speech, and to assemble, to form associations or unions, to move freely throughout the territory, to settle in any part of the country, and to work in any occupation.

Article 26 gives religious denominations the right to establish institutions, manage their own affairs, and acquire property. Article 30 provides that minorities may establish schools of their choice.

Part IV of the Constitution is labeled "Directive Principles of State Policy." Article 38 in this section states that the nation "shall, in particular, strive to minimize the inequalities in income, and endeavor to eliminate inequalities in status, facilities and opportunities..." Article 39 requires and there will be "equal pay for equal work for both men and women," and that "the health and strength of workers, men and women, and the tender age of children are not abused..."

Article 48 states that the nation "shall endeavor to protect and improve the environment and to safeguard the forests and wild life of the country."

Part XII of the Constitution deals with property, finance, contracts, and suits. Articles 265-269 authorize the imposition of taxes according to laws passed by the Parliament. Articles 268 and 269 authorize taxes on the sale and consignment of goods.

Part XIII of the Constitution deals with trade and commerce. Article 301 stipulates that trade and commerce are free in India, subject to other provisions of the Constitution. However, Article 302 states that Parliament may impose restrictions on trade and commerce.

The primary enabling legislation which legalizes company practices in India is *The Companies Act* (modified in 2013).[37] The English version of this law is 294 pages long.

The law recognizes various types of companies that may be registered, each of which has several sub-types. Among those recognized are private and government companies, partnerships, limited liability partnerships, cooperative society, societies, and not-for-profit companies. Companies must have a Board of Directors: "a minimum number of three directors in the case of a public company, two directors in the case of a private company, and one director in case of a One Person Company." The normal maximum is 15 directors (*The Companies Act*, Section 149). No single person may be a director of more than 20 companies.

The Companies Act stipulates ways in which domestic firms may merge with foreign firms and vice versa (Paragraph 234). The Central Government has authority to merge two domestic companies if it is in the national interest (Paragraph 237).

Foreign corporations may register in India. Paragraphs 379-393 of *The Companies Act* give rules for such companies. If 50% or more of a

---

[37]The Companies Act, 2013. The Gazette of India (Extraordinary), Retrieved from http://www.mca.gov.in /Ministry/pdf/CompaniesAct2013.pdf

foreign company is owned by Indian citizens, the company is subservient to various laws of Indian corporations.

Liquidation of a company is no small matter in India. The Companies Act devotes an entire section (Paragraphs 304-365) to this topic. There are additional paragraphs dealing with the liquidation of unregistered companies (Paragraphs 375-378).

The Companies Act in Part C of Schedule II contains a long list giving the useful lives of assets that may be used in calculation of depreciation. Other Schedules provide forms and rules for conducting company business and preparation of company financial statements.

In keeping with national values and thrusts, companies may include in their Corporate Social Responsibility polices activities related to education, promotion of gender equality, eradication of poverty and extreme hunger, improvement of material health, reduction of child mortality, environmental sustainability, and social business development (Schedule VII of *The Companies Act*).

Paragraph 198 of the *Act* shows how profits are to be calculated.

Companies and corporations are legally recognized persons, and must register with the government. Companies and corporations may form subsidiaries which are distinct legal entities.

India allows and encourages foreigners to invest in most Indian enterprises. Joint ventures and wholly owned enterprises are allowed. However, the percentage of ownership of an Indian company by foreigners varies by category. As examples: in medical devices 100% is allowed; in insurance 49%; up to 49% in defense sectors; 100% in construction; petroleum is limited to 49%; and 100% is allowed in certain activities related to railroads. Investment in some sectors requires national government approval. Note there are limitations on investments from citizens of Pakistan and Bangladesh.

Dividends earned in India in foreign-owned enterprises may be repatriated. Investments may normally be repatriated, subject to lock-ins in some sectors.

The national government and the States may impose taxes on individuals and business entities, except the national government may not collect taxes on agricultural income. Residents must pay taxes on Indian income and foreign income. Non-residents must pay taxes on Indian income, but foreign income is not taxable. There is a graduated tax on taxable income ranging from 0% to 30%. Indian corporations must pay 30% tax + additional surcharges on net income earned.

States impose VAT taxes with the rates varying from State to State. Some categories of goods are exempted (mostly basic goods for the

poor); a 4% or 5% rate is common in many States for basic neces-
sity goods, while some States charge as high as 20% for goods such as
cigarettes and imported liquors. Some States have a general VAT tax
rate of 12.5% for uncategorized items.

Contract law is regulated by *India Contract Act* of 1872, with
amendments. The law provides for common contracts as well as many
types of specialized contracts. India has adopted many laws and legal
practices similar to those commonly practiced in the international
community. However, any investor doing business in India is advised
to become very familiar with the details of the Indian current law,
since such details may vary from those of the investor's home country.

India has adopted the *United Nations Convention on the International Sale of Goods (CISG)*. Also, India is a signatory to several international treaties considering intellectual property rights. Included
among these are:

Berne Convention

World Intellectual Property Organization Convention

Trade Related Aspects of Intellectual Property Rights

Paris Convention for the Protection of Industrial Property

World Intellectual Property Organization Convention

Patent Cooperation Treaty (PCT)

Indian law provides for patents, copyrights, and trademarks. Applications for patents may be made by the inventor or the inventor's
legal representative or assignee. Patents have a term of 20 years from
the date on which the patent was applied. Inventions are patentable.
There are exclusions, such as abstract theories, scientific principles,
agriculture methods, and various other categories of inventions.

Copyrights give intellectual property protection to the creators of
original works of authorship. The term of a copyright in India is 60
years from the death of the creator. Copyright protection begins at the
time of creation of the work.

Indian law provides for the registration and legal protection of
trademarks. Services and goods are classified according to the international classification of goods and services.

It behooves each foreign and domestic entity in India to be a watchdog for its own intellectual property. Company surveillance, swift action, and willingness to press one's position in the courts are necessary to diminish the effects of intellectual property theft. It should be

pointed out that the courts in India are notorious for slow action. A court might not hear a case for several years after the case is filed.

Readers are encouraged to determine current Indian laws and to engage an Indian attorney when doing business in India.

JAPAN

Japan has been in existence under various governments for hundreds of years. After being defeated by the United States in World War II, Japan was occupied by the United States which introduced a western-type government. Japan has a population of approximately 127,000,000 people. By land size it is slightly smaller than California. In 2016 the CIA estimated the 2013 Japan Gross National Product on a purchase power basis as US$4.729 trillion. The nation has 47 prefectures. The legal system is based on Civil Law.

The nation's language is Japanese. Over 83% practice Shintoism, 71% are Buddhists, and 2% are Christians.

The Japanese government is a constitutional monarchy with a parliament. The Head of State is the emperor, currently Emperor Akihito. The Emperor's position is a hereditary monarchy.

The country's legislative branch is the Diet, with two houses, the House of Councilors and the House of Representatives. The House of Councilors has 242 members who are elected for six-year terms. The House of Representatives has 480 members who are elected for four-year terms, 300 being in single–seat constituencies and 180 in proportional representation.

The head of government is the Prime Minister who is chosen by the Diet and appointed by the Emperor. At the time of this writing the Prime Minister is Shinzo Abe.

The judicial branch is headed by the Supreme Court which has one chief justice appointed by the Emperor upon recommendation by the Prime Minister's Cabinet. Other justices of the Supreme Court are appointed by the Cabinet.

There are many local and national political parties in Japan. The current Prime Minister, Shinzo Abe, is from the *Liberal Democratic Party*.

Japan is a member of many international organizations, including: the United Nations, the World Bank, the World Trade Organization, and the International Monetary Fund.

The current Japanese Constitution was adopted in 1947 under the leadership of the occupying United States forces. The Constitution is one of the shortest constitutions in the world, the English version of the Constitution being approximately 12 pages long.

The Constitution begins with statements about the Emperor. Article 1 states that the Emperor is "the symbol of the State and of the unity of the people..." Article 2 states that the "Imperial Throne shall be dynastic..." Article 3 states that "The advice and approval of the Cabinet shall be required for all acts of the Emperor in matters of state..." Article 6 states that "The Emperor shall appoint the Prime Minister as designed by the Diet" and "The Emperor shall appoint the Chief Judge of the Supreme Court as designed by the Cabinet."

Renunciation of war is the burden of Article 9. However, in 2015 the interpretation of the Article was modified to allow limited military operations by Japan's military, which is known as the Self-Defense Forces.

"All the people are equal under the law and there shall be no discrimination in political, economic, or social relations because of race, creed, sex, social status or family origin" is given in Article 14.

Articles 19 and 20 establish freedom of conscience, thought and religion. Freedom of speech, assembly, and press are guaranteed by Article 21. Everyone is free to choose and change his or her residence and to choose his occupation provided it supports the public welfare, according to Article 22.

Article 25 states that "All people shall have the right to maintain the minimum standards of wholesome and cultured living" and "the State shall use its endeavors for the promotion and extension of social welfare and security, and of public health."

Articles 27 and 28 deal with workers. "All people shall have the right and the obligation to work." "The right of workers to organize and to bargain and act collectively is guaranteed."

Article 29 protects private property. Article 30 provides for taxation as determined by law.

Article 88 deals with the Emperor again. "All property of the Imperial Household shall belong to the State. All expenses of the Imperial Household shall be appropriated by the Diet in the budget."

Article 98 states that the Constitution is the supreme law of the nation, and Japanese treaties shall be faithfully observed.

With this brief review of the country, the government, and the Constitution, we now move to a consideration of some business practices.

The primary enabling legislation which legalizes company practices in Japan is *The Companies Act* of 2005. The English version of this law is over 500 pages long.

Foreign corporations may register in Japan in various forms. There are four principal company organizations recognized by law. These are:

Gomei Kaisha (GK1). This may be viewed as a partnership in which the partners have unlimited liability.

Goshi Kaisha (GK2). This also may be viewed as a partnership-corporation in which at least one partner has unlimited liability and the other partners have limited liability.

Godo Kaisha (GK3). This form is similar to an LLC in the United States.

Kabushiki Kaisha (KK). This form is owned and run by the shareholders who have limited liability and by directors selected by the shareholders.

The two main forms used in Japan are the GK3 and the KK forms. The KK form is a joint stock company, with governance lodged with the shareholders and the directors. Financial statements must be published. It is more costly to establish than a GK3.

The GK3 is a combination partnership-corporation. It must have at least one partner. Publication of financial statements is not necessary. Profits can be divided among partners by agreement and not necessarily relative to each partner's investment. The GK3 form is relatively new in Japan, so is not so well known as the KK form.

According to *China Go Abroad (www.chinagoabroad.com)*, "foreign companies wishing to have personnel on the ground and living in Japan often prefer to establish a standalone Japanese corporate entity." The two principal options are those described above, the GK3 and the KK.

The Accounting Standards Board of Japan (ASBJ) and the International Accounting Standards Board have been working together for several years to bring convergence of the International Financial Reporting Standards and Japanese GAAP. Some Japanese companies are now allowed to use IFRS principles in their financial reports. The ASBJ is now working with the Accounting Standards Advisory Forum to bring additional direction to the convergence agenda.

The national government and prefectures impose taxes on individuals and business entities. Among these are national and prefecture income taxes, enterprise taxes, property taxes, consumption taxes, and vehicle taxes. The national income tax rates are graduated by taxable income, with rates running from 5% to 40%. Prefecture and municipal income tax rates are 4% and 6% of taxable income, respectively.

The corporate tax rate is now approximately 32%. The present (2015) national government has announced it intends to lower the rate to under 30% in the next five years. Japan's consumption tax rate is now 5% and is scheduled to go to 8% in 2017 and to 10% sometime later.

Contract law is regulated by the *Civil Code*, the *Commercial Code*, the *Consumer Contract Act*, and other laws. The laws provide for common contracts as well as many types of specialized contracts. Japan has adopted many laws and legal practices similar to those commonly practiced in the international community. However, any investor doing business in Japan is advised to become very familiar with the details of the Japanese current law, since such details may vary from those of the investor's home country.

Japan has adopted the *United Nations Convention on the International Sale of Goods (CISG)*. Also, Japan is a signatory to several international treaties considering intellectual property rights. Included among these are:

Berne Convention

Universal Copyright Convention

Agreement on Trade Related Aspects of Intellectual

Property Rights

World Intellectual Property Organization Convention

Patent Cooperation Treaty

Paris Convention for the Protection of Industrial Property

Japanese law provides for patents, copyrights, and trademarks. Services and goods are classified according to the international classification of goods and services. Patents have a term of 20 years from the date on which the patent application was filed. Patents go to the first to file, rather than the first to invent. An invention is patentable provided it is novel, is industrially applicable, does not harm the public good, and other restrictions. There are exclusions, such as products of nuclear reactions or atomic transmutations, or products that harm the public order, public health, or good morals.

Copyrights give intellectual property protection to the creators of original works of authorship. The term of a copyright in Japan is 50 years from the death of the creator. Copyright protection begins at the time of creation of the work.

Japanese law provides for the registration and legal protection of trademarks. Registering a trademark in Japan may take one to two years, if no problems are encountered. Trademarks must be distinctive, so common names of goods, descriptive marks, origin, and place of sale may not receive trademarks. Collective trademarks, such as those used by a business cooperative association, may be registered. Trademarks that are highly recognized outside Japan may receive trademarks in Japan. The term of the trademark is 10 years and may be renewed for another 10 years.

It behooves each foreign and domestic entity in Japan to be a watchdog for its own intellectual property. Company surveillance, swift action, and willingness to press one's position in the courts are necessary to diminish the effects of intellectual property theft.

Readers are encouraged to determine current Japanese laws and to engage a Japanese attorney when doing business in Japan.

MEXICO

The United Mexican States (Mexico) came into existence in 1810 in a revolution which gained the country independence from Spain, after nearly 300 years of Spanish rule. Mexico has a population of approximately 120 million people. By land size it is about three times the size of the U.S. State of Texas. In 2016 the CIA estimated the 2013 Mexican Gross National Product in 2012 on a purchase power basis as US$1.845 trillion. The country has 31 States and a Federal District. Mexico City is in the Federal District and is the capital of the nation.

According to the World Intellectual Property Organization (Retrieved from http://www.wipo.int /pressroom/en/articles/2012/-article_0024.html), "Mexico is the 11th largest world exporter and has the highest value of exports in Latin America, 80% of which are manufactured goods."

Spanish is the principal language of the nation with over 90% of the population speaking only Spanish. About 80% of the population are Catholics. Over 75% of the population is urbanized.

The Mexican government has three branches: executive, legislative, and judicial. The head of state and of government is the President, currently Enrique Peña Nieto. The President is elected by popular vote for a six year term. The President cannot succeed him- or herself.

There is a bicameral Congress consisting of the Senate and Chamber of Deputies. The Senate has 128 members, 96 of whom are elected by popular vote and 32 are allocated based on each party's popular vote. Senators serve a six-year term. The Chamber of Deputies has 500 members, 300 of whom are elected by popular vote and 200 are chosen on the basis of each party's popular vote. Members of the Chamber serve three-year terms. "Senators and Deputies to the Congress of the Union may not be re-elected for the immediately following term" according to Article 59 of the Constitution.

The judicial branch is headed by the Supreme Court of Justice of the Nation, which has 11 justices. The justices are nominated by the President and approved by the Senate. The justices each four years elect one of themselves to be the President of the Court. There is also a Federal Electoral Tribunal and various Federal district courts.

There are many local and national political parties in Mexico. The Institutional Revolutionary Party (PRI) has held national power for most of the nation's history since the Mexican Revolution of 1917. The current President is from the PRI party. Two other prominent parties are the National Action Party (PAN) and the Party of the Democratic Revolution (PRD).

Mexico is a member of many international organizations, including: the United Nations, the World Bank, the World Trade Organization, and the International Monetary Fund.

The current Mexican Constitution was adopted in 1917 and has been amended several times. The English version of the Constitution with its amendments and additions is approximately 130 pages long. It is divided into nine main parts called Titles, which incorporate 136 Articles. In addition there is a Transition section which has 15 Articles, and an Annex with seven Articles. Mexico practices Civil Law.

The Constitution begins with Article 1 which states that "every individual in the United Mexican States shall enjoy the guarantees granted by the Constitution....All discrimination motived by ethnic or national origin, gender, age, handicaps, social condition, health, religion, opinions, preferences, marital status, or any other discrimination that violates human dignity and has the objective of restricting or diminishing the rights and liberties of persons is prohibited."

Article 3 states that "Every individual has the right to receive an education." Further, "education shall be secular..." "All education provided by the State shall be free of charge."

Article 4 provides for various rights. "A man and a woman are equal before the law." "Every person has the right to health protection." "Every family has the right to dignified and decent housing." Every person has a right to food.

According to Article 5, "No person may be prevented from engaging in the profession, industrial or commercial pursuit, or occupation of her or her choice, so long as it is lawful."

Freedom of expression is guaranteed by Article 6. "The expression of ideas shall not be subject to any judicial or administration investigation unless such expression offends good morals, infringes upon the rights of others, incites crime, or disturbs the public order..." Article 7 states that "The freedom to write and publish writings on any subject is inviolable." "The right to assembly or associate peacefully for any lawful purpose shall not be restricted;..." is declared in Article 9. Article 10 gives inhabitants "the right to possess arms in their residences for their protection and legitimate defense, except such as are expressly forbidden by law..."

According to Article 11, "Every man has a right to enter the Republic, exit it, travel through its territory, and change his residence without the need of a security card, passport, or any similar device.

Mexico will not extradite any Mexican citizen to a country if the receiving country would contravene the rights granted by the Mexican Constitution, according to Article 15.

Article 22 states that "Punishment by death, mutilation, infamy, branding, flogging, beating with sticks, torture of any kind, excessive fines, confiscation of property, and any other unusual or extreme penalties are prohibited."

Limited freedom of religion is guaranteed by Article 24. Mexican citizens are free to pursue their religious beliefs. However, religious rites are normally to be conducted inside religious temples. Further, there are limitations on the amount of land religious organizations may own.

Article 26 provides for development of the nation: "The State shall organize a democratic system for the planning of the national development that ensures solidity, dynamism, permanence, and equity of the growth of the economy...'

Individuals can own lands as declared in Article 27. "Ownership of the lands and waters within the boundaries of the national territory is vested originally in the Nation, which has had, and continues to have, the right to transmit title thereof to private persons, thereby constituting private property." "Only Mexicans by birth or naturalization and Mexican companies have the right to acquire ownership of lands, waters, and their appurtenances or to obtain concessions for the exploitation of mines or waters." "Commercial stock companies may acquire ownership of rural lands but only to the extent that is necessary to complete their objective." The State has sovereignty over subsoil rights.

Article 28 establishes the National Bank.

Article 73 gives Congress the right to levy general taxes; to levy special taxes on particular business sectors; to "prevent the establishment of restrictions on interstate commerce;" to "enact laws regarding the planning, promotion, coordination, and execution of actions in the economic field...;" and to enact laws intended to promote Mexican investment, regulate foreign investment, transfer technology, and generate, disseminate, and apply scientific and technical knowledge as required for the national development."

Article 123 gives rights and duties of employers and workers. "The maximum duration of one workday shall be eight hours." "The maximum duration of nighttime work shall be seven hours." "The use of labor of minors under fourteen (14) years of age is prohibited." Pregnant women shall not perform any work that requires considerable effort and presents a danger to their health in relation to their pregnancy;..." "The general minimum wages must be sufficient to satisfy the normal material, social, and cultural needs of the head of a family and to provide for the compulsory education of his children." "Equal wages shall be paid for equal work regardless of sex or nationality." "Workers shall be entitled to a participation in the profits of businesses, regulated..." by norms established by "a national commission composed of representatives of workers, employers, and the government...."

"Wages must necessarily be paid in money of legal tender and cannot be paid in goods, promissory notes, or any other token intended as a substitute for money." "Whenever, due to extraordinary circumstances, the working hours of a day must be increased, the remuneration for the overtime must be paid at the rate of one hundred percent (100%) more than the amount set for normal time. Overtime work may never exceed three hours a day nor three consecutive times. Minors under sixteen (16) years of age may not be admitted to this kind of labor."

Article 123 further requires that "Every agricultural, industrial, mining, or other class of enterprise shall be obligated to furnish comfortable and sanitary accommodations to its workers, it accordance with what is determined by the regulatory law." "The businesses referred to in the first paragraph of this section, which are located away from the centers of population, are obligated to establish schools, clinics, and any other services necessary to the community." "Businesses, regardless of their area of activity, are obligated to provide education or training for the work that they are employed to perform." "Employers shall be responsible for labor accidents and occupational diseases of workers, suffered because of or in the performance of the work or occupation;..."

Article 123 states that "Both workers and employers shall have the right to organize for the defense of their respective interests, by forming unions, professional associations, etc." "The laws shall recognize strikes and lockouts as the rights of workers and employers." "An employer who dismisses a worker without justifiable cause or because he has joined an association or union or has taken part in a legal strike shall be obligated, at the option of the worker, either to fulfill the contract or to indemnify him in the amount of three months' wages."

Important to foreign employers is the requirement that "Every labor contract made between a Mexican and a foreign employer must be legalized by a competent municipal authority and countersigned by the consul of the nation where the worker intends to go, and in addition to the ordinary clauses, the contract shall clearly state that the costs of repatriation of the worker shall be borne exclusively by the contracting employer."

Employers many not require more than one week of work before payment of a day's wages. Employers may not require employees to buy consumer goods in a particular store or place. Employers may not retain wages as a fine.

Property that is the family patrimony is inalienable, cannot be attached or encumbered.

Social security shall provide insurance for old age, life, involuntary unemployment, disability, illnesses, accidents, and day care and other provisions.

Finally, Article 130 requires the separation of church and state.

In 2013 the Mexican government approved an amendment to the Constitution which substantially modified work with petroleum and other hydrocarbons. The new provisions permit the Mexican State to contract with private entities to explore for and extract oil. Private investment will be allowed in oil refining, transportation, and distribution of oil, gasoline, diesel fuel, natural gas, and electric energy.

The primary enabling legislation which legalizes company practices in Mexico is *The Commercial Code of Mexico*. There are two main types of companies in Mexico: Commercial companies and Civil companies. Commercial companies fall under the *Federal Law on Commercial Companies* and Civil companies fill under various *Civil Codes*.

All companies are registered at the Federal level, so companies, corporations, and associations must obtain a permit to incorporate from the national Mexican Ministry of Foreign Affairs. All incorporations must be done through a Mexican notary public and must be registered at the local Public Registry of Commerce. If the corporation intends to allow foreign investments, it must also register at the Federal Registry of Foreign Investment. Other registrations are also required. Companies must register for taxation purposes with the Federal Ministry of Hacienda and Public Credit, with the Federal Institute of Social Security, the national housing authority, and with the national Chamber of Commerce for that company's business sector.

One type of Civil company is the *Sociedad Civil.* This is a company consisting of two or more persons who combine to perform an economic activity, without performing commercial speculation.

Another type of Civil company is the *Asociación Civil.* This is a company consisting of two or more persons who combine to conduct an activity which is non-economic in nature.

Several Commercial types of companies are options for incorporation. The *Sociedad de Responsabilidad Limitada* is a limited responsibility company with a trade name whose partners have obligation to provide their money or assets to the company, which are not represented by negotiable instruments or bearer instruments, the company assets have limited transferability, and other restrictions. There cannot be more than 25 partners.

There is also the *Sociedad en Nombre Colectivo.* This is a company in which all partners have unlimited and joint responsibility for the company's obligation. If a person allows his/her name to be used in the company title, then that person is liable for the company's obligations.

Another type is the *Sociedad en Comandita Simple.* This is also known as a limited partnership. This company consists of one or more partners who are responsible for the company's obligations and one or more silent partners that are responsible for the payment of their portions attributed to the company.

The *Sociedad en Comandita por Acciones* is a silent partnership by stock. This type of company consists of one or more partners/shareholders with joint and unlimited responsibility for the company's obligations and one or more shareholders who are responsible only for the stock they purchase.

The *Sociedad Anónima* is a limited liability stock company with a trade name whose shareholders only have responsibility to provide the costs of the corporate capital which they have purchased. The parts of the company are to be represented by negotiable stock. There must be a minimum of two stockholders. This is a very common business organization in Mexico.

Finally, there are three other types that should be mentioned. The *Asociación en Participación* is established when one or more partners agree to deliver products to a managing partner for use in a business activity. The managing partner performs the business. Both managing and silent partners participate in the profits.

A *Sole Proprietorship* exists when a Mexican national does business in his/her own name without establishing a separate corporation. The sole proprietor is totally liable for all responsibilities of the operation.

A *Business Association* is an organization composed of businesses. If there are 20 or more businesses in the association, they must organize themselves as a national industrial association or chamber.

It is important to the public to know what type of company a given firm is. To this end letters are often placed after the name of the firm to tell the public about the corporate form. The four common forms for business types are: the *Sociedad Anonima* (S.A.); the *Sociedad Anonima De Capital Variable* (S.A. De C. V); the *Sociedad De Responsabilidad Limitada* (S. De. R. L.); and the *Sociedad De Responsabilidad Limitada De Capital Variable* (S. De. R. L. De C. V.) The De C.V. suffix to the names means that the corporation may decrease or increase its capital stock without having to amend its corporation by-law. Most businesses in Mexico are of the S.A. De. C. V. type.

Most economic work in Mexico is open to foreign investors, even 100% ownership. A few sectors are limited to minority participation or completely restricted to foreign investors. Profits may be fully repatriated, as may investments. Profits made in Mexico are subject to Mexican taxation, regardless of the nationality of the owners.

The national government and the States may impose taxes on individuals and business entities. The highest corporate tax rate is currently 30%. It is based on the net income of the company.

Residents must pay taxes on Mexican income and foreign income. The personal income tax rate is also 30%. Non-residents must pay taxes on Mexican income, but foreign income is not taxable. Foreigners may bring money into Mexico without being taxed. There is a sales tax, the IVA, which is charged as a value added tax on most goods and services. The rate is currently 16%.

Contract law is regulated by *Federal Commercial Code of Mexico*, and supplemented by commercial codes of the various states. Specific economic activities have their own special rules, such as maritime, and agrarian activities. Mexico has adopted many laws and legal practices similar to those commonly practiced in the international community. However, there is one principal difference between Mexican contract law and U.S. contract law. In Mexico, a contract does not have to have a consideration. Because of this and other differences, any investor doing business in Mexico is advised to become very familiar with the details of the current Mexican law, and consult a local attorney about any proposed contract.

Mexico has adopted the *United Nations Convention on the International Sale of Goods (CISG)*. Also, Mexico is a signatory to several international treaties considering intellectual property rights. Included among these are:

Berne Convention

World Intellectual Property Organization Convention

Trade Related Aspects of Intellectual Property Rights

Paris Convention for the Protection of Industrial Property

World Intellectual Property Organization Convention

Patent Cooperation Treaty (PCT)

Mexican law provides for patents, copyrights, and trademarks. Patents have a term of 20 years from the date on which the patent was filed. Requirements for patentability are novelty, inventive step, and industrial applicability. Not patentable are biological material found in nature, genetic material found in nature, breeds of animals, new uses of other inventions, and others.

Copyrights give intellectual property protection to the creators of original works of authorship. Normally the creator is the owner of the copyright; however, there is provision in the law for work-for-hire, in which case the commissioners may be viewed as the original owner of the rights. The term of a new copyright in Mexico is 100 years from the death of the creator, but various exceptions occur when the ownership is transferred to another party. Copyright protection begins at the time of creation of the work.

Mexican law provides for the registration and legal protection of trademarks. Mexico is a signatory to the *Madrid Protocol for the International Registration of Marks* as of 2012. Services and goods are classified according to the international classification of goods and services. Under the Madrid system, trademarks may be protected in up to 88 countries with one filing in one country, in one language, with one set of fees.

It behooves each foreign and domestic entity in Mexico to be a watchdog for its own intellectual property. Company surveillance, swift action, and willingness to press one's position in the courts are necessary to diminish the effects of intellectual property theft.

Readers are encouraged to determine current Mexican laws and to engage a Mexican attorney when doing business in Mexico.

NIGERIA

At the time of this writing Nigeria has the largest economy in Africa. The Federal Republic of Nigeria (Nigeria) got its independence in 1960 from the United Kingdom. Nigeria has a population of approximately 175 million people, making it the most populous country in Africa. By land size it is about twice the size of California. In 2016 the CIA estimated the 2013 Nigerian Gross National Product on a purchase power basis as US$478.5 billion. The country has 36 States and the Federal Capital Territory. The capital city is Abuja.

English is the official language of the country, with Yoruba, Igbo, Fulani, and Hausa being principal languages along with 500 others. There are many local and national political parties in Nigeria. There are several hundred ethnic groups. About 50% of the population are Muslims (mostly Sunni), 40% are Christians, and most of the remainder practice a traditional native African religion. Twelve states have majority Sunni-Muslim populations.

The Nigerian government has three branches: executive, legislative, and judicial. The head of state, chief executive, and commander-in-chief of the Nigerian Armed Forces is the President, currently Muhammadu Buhari. The President's term in office is four years and may be renewed once. The President is elected by direct population election. The President's party is the All Progressives Congress Party.

The country's legislative branch, the National Assembly, consists of two bodies, the Senate and the House of Representatives. The Senate has 109 members, three from each of the States and one from the Federal Capital Territory. Members are elected by popular vote and serve four-year terms. The House of Representatives has 360 members who are elected by popular vote and have four-year terms.

Nigeria practices Common Law based on the British model. The judicial branch of government has several Federal courts, including the Supreme Court and the National Federal Court of Appeal. The Chief Justice of the Supreme Court is appointed by the President upon recommendation by the National Judicial Council and confirmation by the Senate. The President of the Federal Court of Appeal is made by the President, upon recommendation of the National Judicial Council, and confirmation by the Senate.

Alongside the customary courts in Nigeria are the Islamic courts which use Sharia law. The Islamic Court of Appeals is recognized at the national level. Sharia is also used for criminal and civil cases in several of the Muslim-majority states. The Sharia Court of Appeal of the Federal Capital Territory is headed by the Grand Kadi, who is appointed by the President, upon recommendation of the National Judicial Council, and confirmation by the Senate. [A Kadi is a judge who uses Islamic law for adjudication]. The Grand Kadi must be an attorney, must have attended and been recognized by an Islamic law institution and held that recognition for at least 12 years; be an Islamic law scholar; and meet other requirements.

The current Nigerian Constitution was adopted in 1999 and has been amended several times. The Constitution is approximately 128 pages long. It is divided into chapters, then parts, and encompasses 320 articles.

The Constitution begins with the statement that "We the people of the Federal Republic of Nigeria Having firmly and solemnly resolved, to live in unity and harmony as one indivisible and indissoluble sovereign nation under God, dedicate to the promotion of inter-African solidarity, world peace, international co-operation and understanding And to provide for a Constitution for the purpose of promoting the good government and welfare of all persons in our country, on the principles of freedom, equality and justice, and for the purpose of consolidating the unity of our people Do hereby make, enact and give to ourselves the following Constitution:"

Article 10 states that "The Government of the Federation or of a State shall not adopt any religion as State Religion."

Article 12 deals with international treaties. No treaty between the Federation and any other country shall have the force of law to the extent to which any such treaty has been enacted into law by the National Assembly."

Article 15(2) deals with discrimination. "....national integration shall be actively encouraged, whilst discrimination on the grounds of place of origin, sex, religion, status, ethnic or linguistic association or ties shall be prohibited." Article 15(3) declares it is the "duty of the State to (c) encourage inter-marriage among persons from different places or origin, or of different religious, ethnic or linguistic association or ties; and (d) promote or encourage the formation of associations that cut across ethnic, linguistic, religious, and or other sectional barriers."

The national economy and economic philosophy are dealt with in Article 16. "The State shall...(a) harness the resources of the nation and promote national prosperity and an efficient, a dynamic and self-reliant economy; (b) control the national economy in such manner as to secure the maximum welfare, freedom and happiness of every citizen on the basis of social justice and equality of status and opportunity"...[and] "protect the right of every citizen to engage in any economic activities outside the major sectors of the economy."

Further, "The State shall direct its policy towards ensuring: (a) the promotion of a planned and balanced economic development, (b) that the material resources of the nation are harnessed and distributed as best as possible to serve the common good, (c) that the economic system is not operated in such a manner as to permit the concentration of wealth or the means of production and exchange in the hands of a few individuals or of a group; and (d) that suitable and adequate shelter, suitable and adequate food, reasonable national minimum living wage, old age care and pensions, and unemployment, sick benefits and welfare of the disable are provided for all citizens."

To regulate business ownership and control, Article 16 also provides that the National Assembly shall be authorized "to review, from time to time, the ownership and control of business enterprises operating in Nigeria and make recommendations to the President on same."

Another article dealing with discrimination in economic and business matters is Article 17. It requires that the "State shall direct its policy towards insuring that: (a) all citizens, without discrimination on any group whatsoever, having the opportunity for securing adequate means of livelihood as well as adequate opportunity to secure suitable employment; (b) conditions of work are just and humane, and that there are adequate facilities for leisure and for social, religious and cultural life;(d) there are adequate medical and health facilities for all persons; (e) there is equal pay for equal work without discrimination on account of sex, or on any other ground whatsoever," and other requirements.

With respect to the environment, Article 20 states that "The State shall protect and improve the environment and safeguard the water, air and land, forest and wild life of Nigeria."

With this brief review of the government and Constitution of Nigeria, we now move to other business related considerations.

Nigeria is a member of many international organizations, including: the United Nations, the World Bank, the World Trade Organization, and the International Monetary Fund.

The primary enabling legislation which legalizes company practices in Nigeria is *The Companies and Allied Matters Act* (1990 and modified). The Act is 35 pages long.

The law recognizes various types of companies that may be registered, each of which has several sub-types. Article 18 states that "any two or more persons may form and incorporate a company by complying with the requirements of this Act in respect of registration of such company." However, "No company, association, or partnership consisting of more than twenty persons shall be formed for the purpose of carrying on any business for profit or gain by the company, association, or partnership, or by the individual members thereof, unless it is registered as a company under this Act, or is formed in pursuance of some other enactment in force in Nigeria."

Article 21 states that "An incorporated company may be either a company (a) having the liability of its members limited by the memorandum to the amount, if any, unpaid on the shares respectively held by them..." or "having the liability of its members limited by the memorandum to such amount as the members may respectively thereby undertake to contribute to the assets of the company in the event of its being wound up..." or (c) not having any limit on the liability of its member..." "A company of any of the foregoing types may either be a private company or a public company."

A private company is defined in Article 22. "A private company is one which is stated in its memorandum to be a private company." "Every private company shall by its articles restrict the transfer of shares." "The total number of members of a private company shall not exceed fifty, not including persons who are bona fide in the employment of the company, or were while in that employment and have continued after the determination of that employment to be, members of the company" and others. Article 24 states that "Any company other than a private company shall be a public company and its memorandum shall state that it is a public company."

There are limited and unlimited companies. An unlimited company must be registered with share capital.

Involvement of companies in politics is controlled by Article 38. "A company shall not have or exercise power either directly or indirectly to make a donation or gift of any of its property or fund to a political party or political association, or for any political purpose..."

Foreign companies wanting to do business in Nigeria must normally incorporate in Nigeria. Article 54 states that "...every foreign
company which before or after the commencement of this Decree was
incorporated outside Nigeria, and having the intention of carrying on
business in Nigeria shall take all steps necessary to obtain incorporation as a separate entity in Nigeria for that purpose, but until also
incorporated, the foreign company shall not carry on business in Nigeria or exercise any of the powers of a registeree company and shall
not have a place of business or an address for service of documents or
processes in Nigeria for any purpose other than the receipt of notices
and other documents, as matters preliminary to incorporation under
this Decree."

Santander https://en.santandertrade.com/establish-overseas /ni-
geria/investing] gives a strong rationale for investing in Nigeria.

> With a population of 160 million people (1/6 of the African population), Ni-
> geria is one of Africa's largest markets. The country has abundant natural
> resources, inexpensive workforce and it is strategically located, with good
> access to many West African countries. Nigeria is also the third largest FDI re-
> cipient in Africa, and the government has been pursuing a policy of economic
> liberalization, promoting public-private partnerships and strategic alliances
> with foreign firms.

According to Santander, the Nigerian government is encouraged
foreign direct investment:

> The Government has introduced many programs to boost FDI, notably in
> agriculture, exploitation and mining, oil and gas extraction, as well as in the
> export sectors. Tax incentives are granted to pioneering industries deemed
> beneficial for the economic development of the country and employment of
> its workforce, such as clothing; allowances facilitating capital investments and
> the deduction of interests on loans for gas companies are also planned. 100%
> foreign ownership of businesses is authorized outside the oil and gas sector,
> where investment is limited to joint ventures or production-sharing agree-
> ments. Industries considered crucial to national security, such as weapons,
> ammunition and military and paramilitary clothing, are reserved for domestic
> investors.

Santander also points out problems with Nigerian investment:

> There are a number of obstacles to FDI: poorly developed transport and en-
> ergy infrastructures, which result in high operating costs; inefficient govern-
> ment institutions and widespread corruption; slow and inefficient judicial
> system and unreliable dispute settlement mechanisms; multiple taxation, re-
> strictive trade policy and increasing lack of security, especially in connection
> with the extremist group Boko Haram operating especially in the north-east
> of the country.

Normally there are no restrictions on repatriation of dividends
earned in Nigeria in foreign-owned enterprises.

The national government and the States may impose taxes on individuals and business entities. Residents must pay taxes on Nigerian income and foreign income. Non-residents must pay taxes on Nigerian income. The company tax rate is 30%. Dividends, interest, rents, royalties, and consultancy fees are taxed at 10%. Individual income tax rates range from 7% to 24%. Capital gains and dividend tax rates are 10%. The VAT tax rate is 5%.

Contract law is regulated by *Law of Contract*. The law provides for common contracts as well as many types of specialized contracts. Nigeria has adopted many laws and legal practices similar to those commonly practiced in the international community. However, any investor doing business in Nigeria is advised to become very familiar with the details of the Nigerian current law since such details may vary from those of the investor's home country.

A legally binding contract according to Nigerian law must have the following five elements: (1) an intent to create a legal relationship; (2) an offer; (3) an invitation to treat; (4) an acceptance; and (5) a consideration.

Nigeria has not adopted the *United Nations Convention on the International Sale of Goods (CISG)*. However, Nigeria is a signatory to several international treaties considering intellectual property rights. Included among these are:

Berne Convention

World Intellectual Property Organization Convention

Trade Related Aspects of Intellectual Property Rights

Paris Convention for the Protection of Industrial Property

World Intellectual Property Organization Convention

Patent Cooperation Treaty (PCT)

Nigerian law provides for patents, copyrights, and trademarks. A creation is patentable if it is capable of industrial application, is new, and comes from creative activity. Patents cannot be obtained for plant or animal varieties or inventions that would go against morality or the public order, scientific principles, and other exclusions. Patents go to the first to file. Patents have a term of 20 years. It should be noted that services and goods are classified according to the international classification of goods and services.

Copyrights give intellectual property protection to the creators of original works of authorship. According to Article 11 of the *Copyright Act*, "The owner of a copyright has the right- *(a)* to claim authorship of his work...To object and to seek relief in connection with any distortion, mutilation or other modification of, and any other derogatory action in relation to his work, where such action would be or is prejudicial to his honour or reputation."Copyright protection extends to 70 years after the lifetime of the creator for literary, musical or artistic works and for 50 years after first broadcast or publication for broadcasts, sound recordings, photography, and some others.

Nigerian law provides for the registration and legal protection of trademarks. It is not necessary to register a trademark; however, if some other entity uses the same trademark you may not have a case for infringement. Trademarks are registered at the Trademarks, Patents and Design Registry in Abuja. Only registered agents can use the online registration process.

It behooves each foreign and domestic entity in Nigeria to be a watchdog for its own intellectual property. Company surveillance, swift action, and willingness to press one's position in the courts are necessary to diminish the effects of intellectual property theft

Readers are encouraged to determine current Nigerian laws and to engage a Nigerian attorney when doing business in Nigeria.

RUSSIA

The Russian Federation (Russia) is the successor state to the Union of Soviet Socialist Republics (USSR), which collapsed in 1991. The Russian Federation consists of Russia and 11 former republics that were part of the USSR. The Russian Federation was fully established by 1993 when the Russian Constitution was adopted.

By land mass Russia is the largest country in the world, almost twice as large as the United States. The population is approximately 145 million. In 2016 the CIA listed the 2013 Russian Gross Domestic Product on a purchase power parity basis as US$2.553 trillion.

The Russian central government has three branches, the executive, legislative, and judicial branches. Heading the executive branch and chief of state is the President of Russia, who currently is Vladimir Putin. The head Chairman of the Government (Prime Minister) is Dmitry Medvedev. Presidential elections are held each four years. The President can serve a maximum of two successive terms. The President appoints the Prime Minister with the consent of the Federal Assembly.

The legislative branch, the Federal Assembly, consists of two chambers, the Council of the Federation and the Duma. The Council of the

Federation has 178 members and the Duma has 450 members. The members of the Federal Council are appointed for a four-year term by the regional units which they represent. Members of the Duma are elected by their regions with a proportional party representation. Terms of office in both chambers are four years.

The judicial branch consists of three central courts, the Constitutional Court, the Higher Arbitration Court, and the Supreme Court. Judges to these three courts are appointed for life. Judges must have a higher education in law and at least five years of law experience.

Russia is a federal state, with various geographic units including 21 republics, 49 provinces, 10 autonomous regions, and two cities of federal status (Moscow and St. Petersburg). These units, called "subjects," have equal status under the Constitution and are subservient to the Russian central administration. They constitute the middle level of government. The third, and lowest level, is the municipality, or local government, such as cities, districts, countries, villages, et cetera. The capital of Russia is Moscow.

The Procurator-General is the highest legal officer of the nation. He or she is appointed by the Council of the Federation upon nomination by the President.

Russia is a member of the United Nations, the World Bank, the International Monetary Fund, and the World Trade Organization.

The English version of the Russian Constitution with its amendments is 33 pages long. It is divided into two sections. Section I has 137 Articles. The second section (two pages long) is divided into nine short sections.

Articles 1 and 3 of the Constitution state that Russia is a federal, law-bound, democratic State with a republican form of government in which the source of power is its multinational people.

Articles 8 and 9 are the enabling statement for basic economic activity. They state that land and other natural resources may be owned by private parties, as well as state and municipal governments. Further, Russia gives guarantees "for the integrity of economic space, a free flow of goods, services and financial resources, support for competition, and the freedom of economic life." Also, "equal protection shall be given to the private, state, municipal and other forms of ownership."

Articles 13 and 14 deal with ideology. Russia is a secular state with no established or obligatory religion. Ideological diversity is recognized.

Article 27 gives citizens and legal visitors the freedom to travel and to reside anywhere in Russia. Article 30 provides for rights of association, including the formation of trade unions. Article 34 provides for each citizen to "a free use cf his abilities and property for entrepreneurial and economic activities not prohibited by law." Articles 35 and 36 give rights of private property, which may be possessed, used and disposed by the individual or in cooperation with other people. Article 37 gives rights of individuals to choose their professions and use their labor as each individual desires.

Article 44 guarantees freedom of "library, artistic, scientific, technical and other types of creative activity, and teaching. Intellectual property shall be protected by law."

Article 68 establishes Russian as the language covering the whole territory. However the Republics may also have their own state languages.

Article 79 gives authority to the Russian state in certain circumstances to participate in international associations and transfer part of its power to these associations according to State treaties.

The primary legal instrument for business practices is the *Russian Civil Code*, which incorporates both civil and commercial law. The *Russian Civil Code* has priority over all laws in the country, except the Constitution. Russia practices Civil Law.

In Russia an individual can participate in entrepreneurial activity without forming a legal entity. However, such a person must register with the appropriate government office. As an example, owners of farms must register with the state.

Business entities are classified in several ways, such as by type (non-profit and commercial), ownership, legal construct, public and private. Legal entities are juridical persons and have various rights and privileges before the law. Foreigners may establish any commercial entity in Russia that is available to Russian citizens.

Foreigners may form business entities, own property, and have 100% ownership, unless prohibited by law in their home countries. Foreign companies may establish subsidiaries and branches in Russia. The legal home of a business is the country in which it is legally established. However, ownership of immovable property such as land and certain movable property, such as cars, is subject to the law of Russia.

The Tax Code provides for various types of taxes, including a VAT and individual income taxes. Russian and foreign organizations with a permanent establishment in Russia or which receive income from Russia pay profit taxes. The corporate tax rate is 30%. Individual income tax rates are 13% on taxable income, except it is 9% on dividends. The VAT rate is 18%, with no VAT on such items as food and medicines.

The *Russian Civil Code* provides laws regarding 28 particular types of contracts. Individuals and juridical persons are free to conclude a contract. Terms of the contract are determined by the discretion of the parties except in cases where the content of the terms is determined by law or legal acts.

Contracts between Russian individuals or parties and foreign persons may choose the country's law to which the contract will be amendable, provided such choice is not subject to a legal prohibition in one of the countries.

The Code recognizes the ownership rights of the creator of intellectual property and provides for state recognition, of patents, copyrights, and trademarks. Russia is a signatory to the *Berne Convention* and several other agreements regarding intellectual property. Inventions, utility models, and industrial designs can be patented in Russia. Russia is a signatory to the *Patent Cooperation Treaty*. Trademarks recognized by the government are valid for 10 years. Trademarks must be used or they may lose their government recognition. Foreigners may register trademarks.

Readers are encouraged to determine current Russian laws and to engage a Russian attorney when doing business in Russia.

SOUTH AFRICA

The Republic of South Africa (South Africa) originated as the Union of South Africa in 1910, then became a republic in 1961. From 1961 until 1994 the country practiced apartheid with white people dominating the country. In 1994 the first multi-racial elections were held which disbanded the apartheid philosophy of government. The present Constitution was adopted in 1996. South Africa has a population of approximately 53 million people. By land size it is approximately twice the size of Texas. In 2016 the CIA estimated the 2013 South African Gross National Product on a purchase power basis as $595.7 billion. The country has nine administrative divisions, called provinces.

There are three capitals. Pretoria is the administrative capital, Cape Town is the legislative capital, and Bloemfontein is the judicial capital.

The nation recognizes eleven languages. About 87% of the population are Christians, with 1.2% being Muslim and 1.2% being Hindu.

The South African government has three branches: executive, legislative, and judicial. The chief of state and head of state is the President, currently Jacob Zuma. The President is elected by the National Assembly. The term of office is five years, with a second term permitted.

The country's legislative branch, the Parliament, consists of two bodies, the National Council of Provinces with 90 members elected by the provincial legislatures, and the National Assembly with 400 members which are elected by popular vote. Members of both bodies have five year terms.

The judicial branch has the Constitutional Court and the Supreme Court of Appeals, and other high courts. The Supreme Court of Appeals consists of a chief Justice, a Deputy Chief Justice and a number of judges determined by an Act of Parliament. The justices are appointed by the President upon consultation with various government bodies. An Act of Parliament determines the terms of the judges.

The Constitutional Court consists of a president, a deputy president, and nine other judges. All judges on the Constitutional Court are appointed by the President after consultation with various government bodies or persons. A Constitutional Court judge serves for one 12-year term. He or she must retire at age 70.

There are dozens of political parties in South Africa. The party of the current President, Jacob Zuma, is the African National Congress, at the time of this writing the ruling party in South Africa.

South Africa is a member of many international organizations, including: the United Nations, the World Bank, the World Trade Organization, and the International Monetary Fund.

The current South African Constitution was adopted in 1996. The English version of the Constitution is approximately 77 pages long. It is divided into 14 chapters with 243 Articles. In South Africa the type of law practiced is mixed, being based on English common law and European Continental law. Article 232 of the Constitution states that "Customary international law is law in the Republic unless it is inconsistent with the Constitution or an Act of Parliament."

The Constitution begins with the a Preamble which states a purpose, among others, of laying "the foundations for a democratic and open society in which government is based on the will of the people and every citizen is equally protected by law." Article 1 states that "The Republic of South Africa is one, sovereign, democratic state founded on the following values: (a) Human dignity, the achievement of equality and the advancement of human rights and freedoms. (b) Non-racialism and non-sexism. (c) Supremacy of the constitution and the rule of law. (d) Universal adult suffrage, a national common voter's roll, regular elections and a multi-party system of democratic government, to ensure accountability, responsiveness and openness."

Article 9 states that all are equal before the law and the state may not unfairly discriminative against anyone on the basis of "race, gender, sex, pregnancy, marital status, ethnic or social origin, colour, sexual orientation, age, disability, religion, conscience, belief, culture, language and birth."

Articles 14-19 guarantee the rights to privacy, religion, belief, opinion, expression, association, and political choice.

Article 23 treats labor relations. Every worker has the right to form and join a union, while every employer has the right to form and join an employers' organization.

Article 26 states that everyone has a right to have access to adequate housing. Article 27 states that all citizens has a right to have access to health care services, including reproductive health care, to sufficient food and water, and to social security, and if they are unable to support themselves and their dependents, to social assistance.

Article 29 states that everyone has a right to a basic education and to receive education in the official language or languages of his or her choice. Further, everyone has the right, at his or her own expense, of establish their own independent educational institution.

Several portions of the Constitution deal with Provincial and local governments. In general, provinces replicate the national government structure. As a general rule, laws passed by the national Parliament have primacy over provincial laws.

Chapter 13 of the Constitution deals with finances. The Constitution authorizes the national government and the provinces to assign taxes in keeping with the national interests. Article 215 requires "national, provincial, and municipal budgets to promote transparency, accountability, and the effective management of the economy...'

Article 223 establishes the South African Reserve Bank as "the central bank of the Republic..."

The primary enabling legislation which legalizes company practices in South Africa is *The Companies Act* of 2008.[38] The English version of this law is 339 pages long. Chapter 2 deals with the formation, administration, and dissolution of companies.

---

[38]*The Companies Act 71 of 2008.* Retrieved from http://www.justice.gov.za/legislation/ acts/2008-071amended.pdf

The law recognizes various types of companies that may be formed. Paragraph 13 of *The Companies Act* states that "One or more persons, or an organ of state, may incorporate a profit company, and an organ of state, a juristic person, or three or more persons acting in concert, may incorporate a non-profit company..." This article gives the two main types of corporations in South Africa, the profit and non-profit corporation.

Non-profit companies are established for the public benefit, such as for religion, science, charity, education, or recreation. Profit companies may be public, a personal liability company, a sole proprietorship, a partnership, or trust.

By Paragraph 23 of *The Companies Act*, "An External company must register...within 20 business days after it first begins to conduct business, or non-profit activities, as the case may be, within the Republic." An external company is a foreign company conducting business, or non-profit activities in the Republic. Paragraph 23 gives several examples of activity that would be considered as conducting business in the country.

Paragraphs 36-48 of *The Companies Act* gives the regulations concerning issuance of shares, classes of shares, and rights and limitations of share terms.

Foreign investors tend to favor a private company form of corporation, which must have at least one director and shareholder and membership of 50 or less. Directors need not be South African nationals or residents.

South Africa provides for domesticated companies, which are foreign companies which have moved their legal registration to South Africa.

As noted above, partnerships are authorized. This is an organization of between two and 20 people who join together to operate a profit business. There are several types of partnerships, including: Commanditarian partnerships, Anonymous partnerships, and Ordinary partnerships.

South Africa encourages investment by foreigners. There are almost no restrictions on the extent of foreign investment. There are many government grant programs that support foreign investment, including: a Foreign Investment Grant, which provides up to 15% of new machinery and equipment value: the Strategic Industrial Project which provides for tax allowances; a Skills Support Program, which grants up to 30% of workers' salaries and up to 50% of training costs; and more.

At the time of this writing, foreign firms may without restriction invest in share capital in African firms. Further, there are few restrictions on repatriating dividends from South African firms to foreign countries.

The national government and the provinces may impose taxes on individuals and business entities. Personal tax rates range from 18% to 41%, although low income persons do not pay personal income taxes. Income earned outside South Africa by South Africans may or may not be taxed depending on the tax status of the individual. There is a VAT tax of 14%.

Corporate tax rates have declined in recent years. At present corporations pay taxes at rates between 0% and 28%. There are special formulas for gold mining companies.

With respect to contract law, South Africa has adopted many laws and legal practices similar to those commonly practiced in the international community. However, any investor doing business in South Africa is advised to become very familiar with the details of the South African current law, since such details may differ from those of the investor's home country.

South Africa is not a signatory to the *United Nations Convention on the International Sale of Goods (CISG)*. South Africa is a signatory to several international treaties considering intellectual property rights. Included among these are:

Berne Convention

World Intellectual Property Organization Convention

Trade Related Aspects of Intellectual Property Rights

Paris Convention for the Protection of Industrial Property

World Intellectual Property Organization Convention

Patent Cooperation Treaty (PCT)

South African law provides for patents, copyrights, and trademarks. Individuals may file for provisional patents. The provision patent provides protection for 12 months. Only patent attorneys may file a non-provisional patent application. If approved, the patents are protected for 20 years from the date of filing of the non-provisional application.

Creative works are eligible for copyright provided they have been produced in some manner. A copyright is automatic and does not require registration. The copyright protection of creative works originating in South Africa has protection in all countries which are signatory to the Berne Convention. The copyright term is normally 50 years from the year of the creator's death. For some creative works the term is for 50 years from first transmission or publication. Anonymous works are protected for 50 years from when the creator is presumed dead, or for 50 years from first publication, whichever is shorter.

Trademarks are registered with the Companies and Intellectual Property Commission. A trademark does not have to be registered, but it can be protected in court only if it has been registered. Once registered, the trademark can be protected indefinitely, but its registration must be renewed every ten years.

With this review of the Constitution and business law, we bring this brief excursion into South Africa to a close. It behooves each foreign and domestic entity in South Africa to be a watchdog for its legal status and its own intellectual property. Company surveillance, swift action, and willingness to press one's position in the courts may be necessary.

Readers are encouraged to determine current South African laws and to engage a South African attorney when doing business in the country.

Resources

Blanchard, K. (2007). *Leading at a Higher Level*. Pearson Prentice Hall

Elgin, C. & Oztunali, O. (2012). Shadow economies all around the world: Model-based estimates.
Retrieved from http://www.voxeu.org/article/shadow-economies-around-world-model-based-estimates

Goldratt, E. (1990). *Theory of Constraints*. Great Bennington, MA: North River Press.

Hagerty, J. (2014). Decimated U.S. Industry Pulls Up Its Socks. *Wall Street Journal*, December 26, p. B6.

Helpman, E. (2011). *Understanding Global Trade*. Cambridge, MA. Harvard.

Hitt, M. A., Ireland, R., & Hoskisson, R. E. (2012). *Strategic Management: Competitiveness and Globalization: Concepts and Cases* (10th Ed.). Independence, KY: Cengage Learning.

Kim, W.C. & Mauborgne, R. (2015). *Blue Ocean Strategy: How to Create Uncontested Market Space and Make the Competition Irrelevant.* Boston, MA: Harvard Business Review Press.

Koch, R. (2011). *Strategy: How to Create, Pursue, and Deliver a Winning Strategy* (4th Ed.). New York, NY: Prentice-Hall.

Lawler, E.E, & Worley, C.G. (2006). *Built to Change: How to Achieve Sustained Organizational Effectiveness*. San Francisco, CA: Jossey-Bass.

Mintzberg, H., Ahlstrand, B., & Lampel, J. (1998). *Strategy Safari*. Prentice Hall Europe.

Pasmore, B. (2015). *Leading Continuous Change: Navigating Churn in the Real World*. Oakland, CA: Berrett-Koehler.

Patel, T. (2014). Cross-*Cultural Management: A Transactional Approach*. London, England: Routledge.

Porter, M. E. (2008). The five competitive forces that shape strategy.

Harvard Business Review, January 2008.

Reuvid, J. (2015). *The business guide to credit management: Advice and solution for cash-flow control, financial risk, and debt management* (2nd Ed). Kogan Page. [First edition is 2010].

The Author

The author of these essays is Samuel Dunn, currently Professor of Business at Northwest Nazarene University of Idaho. Dunn holds the PhD degree in Mathematics and the DBA degree in International Business.

Dunn served as Professor of Mathematics and Business, Dean, and Vice President for Academic Affairs at Seattle Pacific University, then Professor of Business and Mathematics and Vice President for Academic Affairs at Northwest Nazarene University. He is a long-time futurist, with several publications in futurist journals.

After a few years as a professor of mathematics, Dunn moved into academic administration. In that role he viewed himself as a businessperson working in the second largest civilian industry in the United States, which is education. The essays in this book come from his experience as a management leader dealing with opportunities and challenges in a growth industry.

For fun Dunn likes to travel, read, and take Saturday tips with his wife, Lois. At the time of this writing he has been in 53 countries. The Dunns have two grown children; one is a forensic scientist serving in the United States and the other is a medical doctor serving in Asia.

42

TIPS FOR

TOP

GLOBAL

LEADERS

========

In this book you will find leadership insights garnered from 30 years of organizational experience. The author shares with you his observations and advice about methods that work and some that don't work. His careful advice and occasional admonitions will benefit you as provide leadership to for-profit and not-for-profit organizations.

www.ingramcontent.com/pod-product-compliance
Lightning Source LLC
Chambersburg PA
CBHW061335220326
41599CB00026B/5191